HAYAGRĪVA

Other titles by R. H. van Gulik, available from Orchid Press:

Crime and Punishment in Ancient China: *T'ang-Yin-Pi-Shih*

Mi Fu on Ink-stones

Scrapbook for Chinese Collectors: A Chinese Treatise on Scrolls and Forgers

The Lore of the Chinese Lute: An Essay in the Ideology of the Ch'in

R. H. van Gulik biography available from Orchid Press:

Dutch Mandarin: The Life and Work of R. H. van Gulik

馬頭明王古今諸說源流考

HAYAGRĪVA

HORSE CULT IN ASIA

R. H. van Gulik

ORCHID PRESS

R. H. van Gulik
HAYAGRĪVA: Horse Cult in Asia

Second edition, 2005

Originally published as *HAYAGRĪVA: The Mantrayanic Aspect of Horse-Cult in China and Japan*; E. J. Brill, Leiden 1935

ORCHID PRESS
P.O. Box 19,
Yuttitham Post Office,
Bangkok 10907 Thailand
www.orchidbooks.com

Cover illustration: *Hayagrīva with the staff*; thangka painting on cloth, length 194 cm; Tibet, 19th century; collection of the Rijksmuseum voor Volkenkunde, accession number 1383-2.

ISBN 978-974-524-156-5

CONTENTS

LIST OF ILLUSTRATIONS vi
ACKNOWLEDGMENTS vii

CHAPTER I: MAHĀYĀNIC GODS 1

CHAPTER II: HAYAGRĪVA IN INDIA
1. Hayagrīva in Hinduism 9
2. Hayagrīva in Buddhism 22
3. Iconographical Survey 29
A. Hayagrīva as a single god 29
B. Hayagrīva as a secondary god 39

CHAPTER III: HAYAGRĪVA IN CHINA
1. Horse-cult before the introduction of Buddhism 41
2. The Buddhist Hayagrīva 44
3. Hayagrīva in the Chinese Canon 48
A. The reading of the magic formulae 48
B. The mystic gestures of the hands 51
C. Shorter references 54
D. The longer text of the T'o-lo-ni-chi-ching 56

CHAPTER IV: HAYAGRĪVA IN JAPAN
1. Horse-cult before the introduction of Buddhism 76
2. The Buddhist Hayagrīva 79
3. Hayagrīva in the Japanese Canon 81

CHAPTER V: CONCLUSIONS 95

ENDNOTES 97
INDEX 98

LIST OF ILLUSTRATIONS

		Facing Page (unless noted)
I	Hayagrīva, Lakṣmīnarasiṁha Temple	22
II	Hayagrīva, Lakṣmīnarasiṁha Temple	23
III	Hayagrīva, popular image	32
IV	Hayagrīva embracing his çakti	33
V	Hayagrīva with the staff (Leiden Museum, 1383-2)	34
VI	Hayagrīva with the Iron-Sword	(in text) 36
VII	Mysterious Hayagrīva	(in text) 36
VIII	Hayagrīva as summoned by Atīça	(in text) 37
-	Hayagrīva in the form of a Magic Dagger (*phur bu*)	(in text) 38
IX	Hayagrīva of Tjandi Djago	35
X	Hayagrīva as represented in the Taizōkai	80
XI	Hayagrīva sitting on a rock	81
XII	Hayagrīva with staff and Lotus-flower	82
XIII	Hayagrīva on the water-buffalo	83

ACKHOWLEDGMENTS

This paper was presented in order to obtain a doctor's degree at the University of Utrecht. I wish here specially to thank Thos. T. H. FERGUSON, professor of Chinese at the above-mentioned University, and Dr. J. RAHDER, professor of Japanese at the University of Leyden. Prof. FERGUSON carefully verified my Chinese translations, and Prof. RAHDER kindly granted me the use of his splendid buddhological library.

After this paper had been printed, I received an appointment at the Netherlands Legation in Tōkyō. If I had known beforehand that I would be able so soon to study my subject on the spot, I would have left out the last chapter, Hayagrīva in Japan. As it is, it must stand, as a preliminary review.

I avail myself of this opportunity to tender my best thanks to Dr. B. BHATTACHARYYA, Director of the Oriental Institute, Baroda, for the valuable information he was kind enough to send me. I feel much indebted to Dr. A. FONAHN at Oslo, who kindly sent me photographs of parts of the Tibetan Canon; to Dr. H. N. RANDLE of the India Office, London, who had some photographs made of Indian palmleaf-manuscripts; and to Mlle M. LALOU, of the Bibliothèque Nationale, Paris, who was good enough to send me some Tibetan sādhana's.

Utrecht, 8—III—1935

Nindasi yajñavidher ahaha çrutijātaṁ
Sadayahṛdayadarçitapaçughātaṁ
Keçava dhṛtabuddhaçarīra
Jaya jagadīça hare

Gītagovinda, I, i

CHAPTER I

MAHĀYĀNIC GODS

. . . bahavaç ca vighnāḥ.
Pañcatantra.

In his endeavour to approach a higher, unknown and unknowable Power, mankind has found in the Idol and in the Word the two most significant symbols. The Idol is the outcome of a definite choice out of the various phenomena of the visual world; in this chosen image a specific aspect of the mysterious Power is considered to be embodied. The Word, on the other hand, is a special but involuntary combination of a few of the many sounds to be distinguished by the ear, which combination then implies a special meaning.

As forms of expression of a higher Power, the Idol and the Word are therefore identical. Religious feeling has always sensed this identity, both in its philosophical aspect, which finds its expression in a combination like Logos and Theos, and in its magical aspect, to which in India a special branch of Northern Buddhism has been devoted.

Perhaps this similarity between Idols and Words is the cause of both having been subjected to vicissitudes so variegated and incalculable, that it will in most cases prove to be impossible, given the form and meaning which we now find inherent to either of them, to arrive at a complete semantic reconstruction of the world of thought which was embodied in an Idol or in a Word. Suppose, for instance, that a word is taken over from one language into another and that the meaning, the conception it conveys, or, in short, the whole world of thought which it connotes, has been entirely altered through misapprehension or local adaptation. If then in the course of time the word should be found to be in use in both languages, it will be generally possible to state for a fact which language has been the borrower; but a very scholarly and painstaking research would be required for the reconstruction of the semantic history which is attached to this fact. This is only an example of a very simple case; generally the problem is much more complicated.

At least as complicated is the semantic research concerning an Idol. In linguistics one can at least count on relatively concrete data, such as, for instance, texts from different periods in which a word occurs in various connections. But in the search after the history of the conceptions which are symbolized by an Idol, even comparative data afford insufficient support. One must pick a way through a labyrinth of subtle associations and conjectured tendencies, in which cause and effect can hardly be distinguished, since everything here is born of the subconscious, which stands quite outside the ordinary pale of intellect and logic. The number of possibilities obtaining here is stupendous. Suppose for instance that in a certain culture-area an Idol is met with, which in different periods is connected with diametrically opposite conceptions. In such a case it may be proved that one has to deal with a quaint evolution of one and the same idea, which evolution may then have been caused by cultural or sociological factors, as when a nomadic people would take to agriculture, etc. But it could also be, that such a thorough divergence in the conception attached to an Idol might be ascribed to the fact that through various circumstances this Idol became the embodiment of two originally quite different ideas: in the first place the idea with which the image was originally connected in a certain culture-area, and secondly the underlying thought of another god in quite another culture-area, at some later date introduced in the former area through political agencies, such as for instance enemy invasion. Owing to the fact that the native Idol happened to bear a name more or less similar in sound perhaps, or more or less resembled the intruding Idol in appearance, it was apt to be looked upon as the same in character and function, and after some time even to be quite supplanted by the new Idol. And here again we have stated only two of a long series of possibilities.

From the above it follows that it is impossible to embrace the nature of an Idol entirely in a single definition. We can not say, for instance: "X. is a God of Thunder", but at the most we can say "in such and such a time and place, X. was looked upon as a God of Thunder". This applies equally to the religions of a highly cultured people as to the religions of peoples of a more archaic order; even more so to the first-named, where there exists a stronger tendency towards limitation and definition, with a consequent loss of minor deviations or special traits, which might have been of much aid to the investigator in the course of his research.

In commencing my study on the Mantrayānic aspect of the god Hayagrīva it seemed incumbent upon me to make the above express reservation.

The Mantrayāna is one of the many later forms of development of northern Buddhism, which are usually indicated by the name Tantrism. It appears to me, however, better not to use the word Tantrism in this study; for since nobody knows exactly what it means, it is apt to cause much confusion. Most modern scholars therefore never use the word without adding an observation as to its vague meaning. Some late-Çivaist works, in which the worshipping of the female energy of the god was brought into strong prominence, bore the very general name of Tantra, a word which by itself does not mean more than a theoretical, scientific work (or a chapter thereof), a collection of instructions or rules (cf. for instance *Kā-tantra*, *Pañca-tantra* etc.). From this word the term Tantrism was deduced, which at the same time came to be applied to çāktic tendencies in later Buddhism, and soon afterwards was used in Buddhology and elsewhere to denote anything relating to religious erotics or black magic. For a long time it remained a danger signal marking off an uncouth territory to all decent people. In reality the word is thus a remnant from the initial stages of Mahāyānic studies in the West, when only very little was known of the later forms of development of Buddhism. Even now the field which has been opened out by the assiduous application of some devoted investigators[1]) remains but small against the vast regions which are still unexplored. But we have in any case proceeded so far that behind the tract of land marked off by the inscription "Tantrism" we know of vast regions which are distinguished from each other by very marked features. Hence the word Tantrism, which used to denote an unknown entity for the want of better, might now well be dropped out of Indology entirely; for what was supposed to be an entity is now proved to consist of a great many very heterogeneous parts which can no longer be joined into one conception without falling into errors of undue generalization or giving rise to confusion. On the other hand each of the component parts may be denoted by its own usually very expressive name, e.g. Çaiva-siddhānta, Vajrayāna, etc.; and in case one should wish to characterise in general terms the later forms of development of Hinduism and Buddhism together, one might use expressions like syncretic-magical, or some term to the same effect. In how far the word Tantrism might be maintained in ethnology in its arbitrary meaning of the religious-erotic is a question which would have to be considered as a matter standing by itself.

Of those many later forms of development of the Mahāyāna we shall here only give our particular attention to the Mantrayāna, for it is in this system that the god Hayagrīva has figured to a predominating extent, especially outside of India.

Mantra means magic incantation or formula and as such has been defined as "power in the form of sound"[2]). Yāna (litt. vehicle) is a means of crossing the sea of rebirths and attaining to Salvation; it is the usual term employed to denote a certain

---

1) BHATTACHARYYA, DE LA VALLÉE POUSSIN "AVALON" (Sir JOHN WOODROFFE) and others.

2) Cf. A. AVALON, The Serpent Power, London 1931, p. 84.

trend of Buddhism. Hence Mantrayāna is the method through which one can reach Salvation by muttering certain words and phrases. The roots of this curious system may be traced back to very old, probably even pre-Indo-Aryan days. The belief in the power of the magic formulae plainly evinces itself in many cantos of the Atharva-veda such as the ābhicārikāṇi, curses and incantations against demons, sorcerers and enemies generally [1]). This belief seems to be particularly rooted in the propensity towards magic existing among the ancient aboriginal tribes of India. Many of these ancient conceptions were adopted by the Indo-Aryan conquerors and made an integrant part of their own conceptions. In different parts of India, however, situated outside the centra of Indo-Aryan culture, where the aboriginal population was better able to preserve its own character, the native usages of magic and witchcraft maintained themselves in a form more closely resembling the pristine.

When now in the 3d to 8th century A.D. the Mahāyāna extended itself over these tracts as well, conquering all foreign elements by the simple process of absorbing them, we find it also incorporating amongst others these early conceptions in magic. Probably for a great part also as a reaction against the many involved philosophical systems, cast in an entirely Indo-Aryan mould, which at that time held great sway, these magical conceptions came to fill an important part; so much so, that they were soon adopted and assimilated into the Indo-Aryan system. On strength of this we now find this magic lore acquiring, *more Indico,* next to its secular aspect of procuring all sorts of material advantages through immaterial means, also a hieratic aspect in the shape of a well-defined philosophical system, the Mantrayāna.

This method of Salvation rests on the theory that man even in his earthly body, which is built up out of the five elements, can reach Buddhahood, and therefore every human being in this life is potentially a Buddha. For the attainment of this state, which means Salvation, it is not necessary to subject oneself to a strenuous discipline carried on through many existences; the reciting of a certain formula, accompanied by the corresponding posture of the hands is sufficient. Here we thus find the word restored to its ancient, holy function, the form of expression *par excellence* of the all-highest Power.

As such it stands on a foot of equality with the Idol, or even above it, for though these images may bring Salvation to the supplicant, they must first be worshipped according to special and extremely involved rites, of which prayer and incantation again

---

1) Cf. also the Ṛg-veda hymns VII, 55 and 104.

form an integral part. The mantra, on the other hand, is the short cut leading directly to the goal. This omnipotence of the word finds expression in manifold ways. The image of a god, for instance, is only held to be animated with its mystic life after some mantra's, written on a piece of paper or on a wooden tablet, have been placed inside it. In Tibet the cavity in which these mantra's are placed is accordingly called "mantra-place" [1]). Care is also taken to write votive formulae on the reverse of paintings of gods and saints at the spots corresponding to their vital parts.

The consequence of this great power of the word is that in the Mantrayāna the Gods, which under the influence of their identification with local deities often came to be looked upon in a very material and therefore individual way, now resumed their higher, abstract signification, and returned to their original value as symbols. In the Great Magic Circle of the Mantrayāna this idea is given plastic form by representing all Idols taken up therein as emanations from the central figure Vairocana, whose mystic germ consists of the sound *a*, the mother of all sounds according to the most ancient conceptions.

Finally I should like to add a few words on the iconographic history of the Mantrayāna. At the time of the rise of the Mahāyāna the "three worlds" were already peopled with hosts of gods and godlings. The origin of this apparent multiplicity must be looked for in the fact that the entire Indian philosophy of life is based on the conviction that the all-highest Power is present equally in all things. This conviction has been very pithily expressed in the well-known formula tat tvam asi, "that art thou". The belief in this all-pervading life gave to its votaries a remarkable power of abstraction on one side and of personification on the other. "There is no limit to a pantheon where hope, hell and hunger, cows and corn, the west and wisdom, etc., are all called gods" [2]). In its deeper sense this is a consequence of not recognising any distinction between mind and matter. Mind is the only reality, outside of which nothing can exist. In the stylistic figures of Sanskrit we find this thought clearly reflected. Thus for instance one would say of a sword that it is as hard as the heart of a cruel man. We occidentals always reverse the order and use the concrete first to illustrate the abstract. As a typical example might be quoted the lines in Kālidāsa's drama Vikramorvaçī, where in the fifth act the Chamberlain says to the King, whose arrow had transfixed a bird which had stolen a jewel from him: "This bird has been killed by thy anger, which has turned into an arrow" (*roṣeṇa te*

---

1) Cf. SCHLAGINTWEIT, Buddhism in Tibet, London 1863, p. 206.

2) Cf. E. WASHBURN HOPKINS, Epic Mythology, Strassburg 1915, page 53.

mārgaṇatāṅ gatena). From this passage one sees clearly that to the Indian mind no definite boundary exists between mind and matter. As usual, delicate psychic shades find here also a faithful mirror in the language.

Although in the different yāna's of Northern Buddhism the philosophical background of the world of the gods is often formulated in a different manner, yet all these conceptions ultimately rest on the above described principle of the all-pervading life. Hence Mahāyāna could so easily absorb gods from other systems. Thus it has taken over, with or without adaptations, most of the gods in the Hindu pantheon into its own system, where their ranks go to increase the multitude of special Buddhist Saints and Gods. It also adopted many local gods and probably even figures from foreign (the Near-East) systems. Thus the Mahāyāna with its various schools could develop into a remarkable synthesis of elements culled from the most widely different sources. Now in the Mantrayāna these almost unlimited numbers have been arranged somewhat more systematically. Besides being classed under families (*kula*) they are now also combined into the different categories formed by the mystic worlds (*dhātu*), fixed groups which are graphically represented in the Circles of Meditation (*maṇḍala*). These are, as it were, esoteric plans where every god, every satellite, occupies his own special place. But through this very endeavour to systematize new gods are born for whose origin it is now no longer necessary to search for deep-seated causes. Thus some new god, with his specific, minutely described attributes and his own magic formula, may come into being merely in order to occupy the fourth corner of an altar, to make an odd number even, to complete the scheme of colours, to bring symmetry to two groups, etc. etc. And all these countless gods may mate with their female counterparts to give birth to again new generations of gods.

Supposing now that a study has to be made of the real significance and nature of a certain figure out of this stupendous pantheon in China one will have to take into account all the different sources which may have contributed to the long history of its development. In the first place it will be necessary to make sure whether one has to do with an Indian god imported with the Mantrayāna, or with a native god from China which has been incorporated locally into the Mantrayāna, or Mahāyāna in general. Should the first supposition prove to be the correct one, it is necessary to find out whether the god in question was originally a Hindu god, or belonged to Buddhism. In the first case one should find out in how far the significance of the god has been altered by its transfer to Buddhism. This is an important point, for some Hindu gods have been entirely degraded, while others experienced material promotions, and others again remained pretty well on the same level [1]). Should, on the other hand, the figure prove to be an original Buddhist god, it will be necessary, in case the origin cannot be traced directly (as, for instance, in the many cases in which the god is a personification of a philosophic conception), to trace its history as far back as possible. This will often bring one on to tracks leading to territories situated outside the Indo-Aryan culture-area.

Having thus traced the figure, also from an iconographic point of view, down to its original Indian shape, one will have to return to China again in order to compare the significance and external shape of the figure in China with the result of the foregoing study, in order to establish the changes in the figure which took place during the transfer. To be able to do so we have first to make sure whether perhaps a similar figure was already in existence in China and in how far this figure may have influenced the Buddhist conception or may have been merged into it. This is a complicated question. By itself a phantastically extended system, the Mantrayāna has always, wherever it came, drawn freely from native sources. Only by this show of liberality could it gain a footing in a country like China, where tradition stood so firm. Through this far-reaching process of blending, the Chinese Mantrayāna has grown into an edifice which presents a perplexing aspect to the student who wishes to analyse it in its component parts. And equally perplexing as the religious system is the art which was inspired by it, as evinced in the ornamentation of the walls of Mantrayānic temples and monuments in China. It is a puzzling, but therefore none the less picturesque beauty, which in its bold mingling of

---

1) As to the attitude of the Buddhist sects generally towards the gods of the Hindu-pantheon, B. BHATTACHARYYA says: "The attitude of the Buddhist priests towards Hindu religion and its gods and goddesses was entirely unfavourable, if not antagonistic. They were not only hostile to the Hindu gods, but their hostility proves further that they had a great hatred towards the members of other religions also...." (in: An Introduction to Buddhist Esoterism, Oxford 1932, p. 116; his point of view can be found more fully discussed in his edition of the Sādhanamālā, II, p. CXXX). Amongst others he cites as examples that many Buddhist gods hold up a head of Brahmā, or crush Gaṇeça underfoot. A. K. COOMARASWAMY protested against this in the Journal of the American Oriental Society, vol. 46, p. 188, and gives quite a different interpretation of the two cases cited above. Truth probably is equally divided between the two. It can not be denied that Buddhists often pictured the Hindu gods in word or image in a humiliating or derogatory way. But on the other hand one often finds the same gods represented by them in their full dignity. Thus on Tibetan pictures one often sees Gaṇeça crushed by a Mahāyānistic god; but the same Gaṇeça is seen enthroned with all his usual attributes on Tibetan bronze lamps. Hence it is evidently a case of an incidental symptom, viz. local or sectarian spasms of Hindu-phobia on one side, where Buddhism wanted to emphasize its own character, alternating on the other hand with more conciliatory frames of mind. The farther one is removed from the hearth of Hindu-culture, the more one finds the latter attitude prevailing.

the most widely divergent plastic elements, its quaint combinations of the enticing and the terrible, puts all description to shame.

In Japan the Mantrayāna was finally brought into the most systematic form and rounded off into a self-contained system, which constituted the tenets of the Shingon-sect. But again one has to take into very good account the original Japanese Shintō-elements, which here also have made their influence felt to a considerable extent.

Finally we must not exclude Tibet from our explorations either, as in the Tibetan Canon rich material has been preserved, which besides amplifying and completing the Indian data, presents in itself an enthralling field of research. Moreover, through the ages there has been a rich interchange of cultural data between that country and China, so that a study of Lamaism is indispensable for a right understanding of Chinese Buddhist art and letters.

Although in this study of the god Hayagrīva I have taken China as a starting-point, it appeared to me logically and historically more correct to preface the chapter on China by a review of this deity in India, after which I have furthermore taken a rapid glance at the Tibetan data. For the sake of completeness I had to add a few remarks on the occurrence of images of Hayagrīva found in Further-India and in Java.

I have tried to view this figure in as broad a light as possible, and attempted to fathom its semantic history. It goes without saying, however, that the material I could utilize for my study of this subject was insufficient to ensure a complete success of the endeavour, which in the first place would have necessitated a lengthy search for more realia in Indian and Chinese libraries. When these materials could have been brought together, and when on the base of these, the many general problems connected with the history of the Mantrayāna could have been elucidated, then only one might hope to be able to make a thorough study of Hayagrīva and many other deities, whose semantic history finely illustrates the development of religious thought in all countries where Northern Buddhism was introduced. This paper can not be more than a preliminary review of the territory to be explored, only suggesting some clues that might be followed up. I would, however, consider my effort richly recompensed if it should appear that through this study of mine of the sources here available, I have at least been able to smooth the way for further research.

CHAPTER II

HAYAGRĪVA IN INDIA

1. Hayagrīva in Hinduism

samāmnāyaḥ samāmnātaḥ; sa vyākhyātavyaḥ.
YĀSKA

In the old Indogermanic conceptions the horse has taken an important place. It was regarded as being most closely connected with the sun, and as such must have played a large part in all fertility and fecundity rites. These facts are evident in greatly varying sources. In the Nordic bronze-culture the horse appears about 1000 B.C., represented as pulling along the disc of the sun [1]. This representation is under the influence of Southern Europe, even though the idea itself was undoubtedly immediately taken to the North by the Indogermanizing conquerors. The same conquerors have introduced the cult of the sun and the sun-steed into all the territories occupied by them [2].

Therefore it goes without saying that among the Indo-aryan conquerors who invaded the fruitful Land of the Seven Rivers about 2000 B.C., the horse stood in high esteem. The material which is at our disposal in the Veda's is indeed too heterogeneous to allow one to form a sharply outlined definition of the significance of the horse in the Vedic period. For all that it is apparent from more than one passage in the Veda's that the horse was brought into relation with the sun. A special horse-god is lacking to be sure, but all horses mentioned by name appear to be more or less identified with the sun. The most speaking example is the steed Dadhikrā (Dadhikrāvan) which is sung of in several hymns of the Ṛg-veda (IV, 38:2, 3, 5, 10; 40:2, 3; VII, 44:4). From these and other passages (Ṛg-veda, I, 163:2; VII, 77:3) it will be clear that the horse was especially connected with the sun [3].

1) Cf. SOPHUS MÜLLER, Urgeschichte Europas, Strassburg 1905, p. 116, especially the picture.

2) It is not necessary to dwell at length upon the facts relative to this subject. In the standard works on archaeology and prehistory one may find all the material collected. Cf. i. a., E. WAHLE, Deutsche Vorzeit, Leipzig 1932, index s. v. Pferd; H. GÜNTERT, Der Ursprung der Germanen, Heidelberg 1934, p. 49 sq. For the horse-sacrifice cf. K. F. JOHANSSON, Ueber die alt-indische Göttin Dhiṣanā und Verwandtes, Uppsala 1917, p. 108 sq.; W. KOPPERS, Die Religion der Indogermanen in ihren kulturhistorischen Beziehungen, Anthropos XXIV (1929), p. 1073 sq., and especially p. 1077 sq.

3) Cf. also MACDONELL, Vedic Mythology, 1897, p. 149—150; Jarl CHARPENTIER, Die Suparṇasage, Untersuchungen zur altindischen Literatur- und Sagengeschichte, Uppsala 1922, especially p. 323, where Tārkṣya is discussed.

In how far one could speak of a definite identification is difficult to say. The language of the Vedic bards rose too quickly to daring poetical comparisons and ecstatic identifications to enable one to draw any conclusive arguments from it. The later Indians, however, (and this is most important for our subject) understood these passages in a literal sense, and considered the divine horse as the sun. By degrees the signification of the horse as symbol of the sun and the idea of fruitfulness became more extensive. Its significance as a fertility and fecundity symbol culminated in the great horse-sacrifice, the Açvamedha[1]) (which in its origin goes back to Ur-Indogermanic fertility-rites; cf. note on page 9).

It is in the epic period that one first finds the word Hayagrīva. It is connected with various ideas, which I shall deal with separately.

The most prominent is the word Hayagrīva as epitheton of Viṣṇu. After the above considerations regarding a general conception of the connection between sun and steed, the existence of this relation need not astonish us. Viṣṇu indeed is in the Vedic period probably, and later on surely, the sun itself. From the variants Açvaçīrṣa, Hayaçīrṣa, Açvamukha, Vaḍavāmukha appears that in this case Hayagrīva ought to be translated as the "Horse-headed One".

Viṣṇu with the horse's head is the reader and the promulgator of the sacred Veda's. In Mahābhārata V, 99, 5[2]) Nārada describes the town Patālā, which lies in the middle of the world of the snakes (*nāga*). He then says: "Here on every auspicious occasion the Horse-headed-one, the āditya, rises and fills the world that is called Suvarṇa, with Vedic hymns" (*atrādityo hayaçirāḥ kāle parvaṇi parvaṇi / uttiṣṭhati suvarṇākhyaṁ vāgbhir āpūrayañ jagat*). And in Mah. XII, 127, where the name Hayaçīrṣa is alternated with Açvaçiras, an Ṛṣi tells about a beautiful region called Badarī, the abode of Nara and Nārāyaṇa: "where, o King, Açvaçiras reads the eternal Veda's" (*yatra cāçvaçirā rājan vedān paṭhati çāçvatān*). In this rubric one must also classify the identification of Viṣṇu with the horse Uccaiḥçravas in Mah. VI, 34, 27, where Viṣṇu praises himself in the presence of Arjuna with the words: "Know me as Uccaiḥçravas among horses, born of nectar, as Airāvata among the best of elephants, and the King among men" (*uccaiḥçravasam açvānāṁ viddhi mām amṛtodbhavaṁ/airāvataṁ gajendrāṇām narāṇām ca narādhipam*). The word Uccaiḥçravas is namely interpreted as "the loudly-roaring one". Thus one may form a

1) Cf. P. E. DUMONT, L'Açvamedha, description du sacrifice solennel du cheval dans le culte védique, d'après les textes du Yajurveda blanc, Paris 1927.

2) Bombay Edition.

connection between the promulgation of the Veda's and this name. But perhaps one ought also to remember another association, namely that of the foaming sea, and then see Viṣṇu as "the sun-horse, rising from the ocean" [1]), although this view appears to me to be less probable. This horse Uccaiḥçravas, the white horse of Indra, is counted among the Seven Treasures (*sapta-ratnāni*) of a World-dominating King (*cakravartin*). The epitheton *amṛtodbhava* refers to its being produced at the churning of the Ocean. In the next chapter we shall see how in Northern Buddhism this idea was further developed.

Another aspect of the horse's head also takes us to the sea: besides being a sweet-voiced singer it is also a fire-spitting swallower. In Mah. XII, 340 Viṣṇu appears before the ascetic Nārada and says: "In the shape of the Horse-headed-one in the north-western ocean I drink good offerings to the gods and oblations to the Manes brought with devotion" (*ahaṁ hayagrīvo bhūtvā samudre paççimottare / pibāmi suhutaṁ havyaṁ kavyañ ca çraddhayānvitaṁ*). A more detailed description is given in Mah. XII, 342, 60: "Formerly Nārāyaṇa was for the benefit of mankind the great Ṛṣi called Vaḍavāmukha. While doing ascese on the mount Meru the ocean was summoned by him. And when it did not come, the ocean was by him, who was angry, transformed into liquid water by the glow of his own body. And at the same time he made the ocean to be salt like his own sweat. He said to the ocean: You will be undrinkable, and then only your water will be sweet when it is drunk by him who is called Vaḍavāmukha. Thus this water is drunk, according to this decision by him who is called Vaḍavāmukha" (*nārāyaṇo lokahitārthaṁ vaḍavāmukho nāma purā maharṣir babhūva / tasya merau tapas tapyataḥ samudra āhūto nāgatas tenāmarṣitenātmagātroṣmaṇā samudraḥ stimitajalaḥ kṛtaḥ svedaprasyandanasadṛçaç cāsya lavaṇabhāvo janitaḥ / uktaç cāpy apeyo bhaviṣyasy etac ca te toyaṁ vaḍavāmukhasaṁjñitena pepīyamānaṁ madhuraṁ bhaviṣyati / tad etad adyāpi vaḍavāmukhasaṁjñitenānuvartinā toyaṁ samudrāt pīyate*). Another representation is that this Vaḍavāmukha is a manifestation of Aurva; the fire which he spits out is then called Aurvānala [2]).

Mah. XII, 347, describes how Viṣṇu as the Horse-headed-one brings back the stolen Veda's, and kills the thieves, two asura's. This story seems to me to be a later extension of the motif of Viṣṇu who with a sweet voice recites the Veda's: he is not only the promulgator of the Veda's, but also their special protector, who restores them whenever they are lost. By this incident Brahmā is represented absolutely subordinate to Viṣṇu. The story goes as follows. Two powerful demons, Madhu and Kaiṭabha, steal the Veda's

1) E. Washburn Hopkins, Epic Mythology, Strassburg 1915, p. 203.

2) Hopkins, op. cit., p. 180.

from Brahmā, and dive with their booty into the ocean. Brahmā implores the aid of Viṣṇu, who awakes from his slumbers, and decides to bring back the Veda's. "Then he awoke from his sleep, determined to obtain the Veda's. Applying his divine power he assumed a second form. Then, shining like the moon, with a beautiful nose, and having assumed a magnificent horse's head, the Lord went to the place where the Veda's were hidden. His head was the firmament with the lunar mansions and the stars. And his hair was long, radiating like the rays of the sun. His ears were the atmosphere and the underworld, his forehead was the earth. The Ganges and the Sarasvatī were his hips, his eyebrows the two great oceans. The moon and the sun were his eyes, while his nose is said to have been the twilight. The sound oṁ was his notion, the lightning was his tongue, and his teeth, o King, are said to have been the Fathers wo drink the Soma. The Goloka and the Brahmaloka were the lips of the exalted one. And his neck, o King, was the Night of Doom, that exceeds the three guṇa's. Having assumed this horse's head, having various forms, the Lord that rules all entered the nether world" (*jahau nidrām atha tadā vedakāryārtham udyataḥ / aiçvaryeṇa prayogeṇa dvitīyāṁ tanum āsthitaḥ / sunāsikena kāyena bhūtvā candraprabhas tadā / kṛtvā hayaçiraḥ çubhraṁ vedānām ālayam prabhuḥ / tasya mūrdhā samabhavad dyauḥ sanakṣatratārakā / keçāç cāsyābhavan dīrghā raver aṁçusamaprabhāḥ / karnāv ākāçapātāle lalāṭam bhūtadhāriṇī / gaṅgā sarasvatī çroṇyau bhruvāv āstām mahodadhī / cakṣuṣī somasūryau te nāsā saṁdhyā punaḥ smṛtā / oṁkāras tv atha saṁskāro vidyuj jihvā ca nirmitā / dantāç ca pitaro rājan somapā iti viçrutāḥ / goloko brahmalokaç ca oṣṭhāv āstāṁ mahātmanaḥ / grīvā cāsyābhavad rājan kālarātrir guṇottarā / etad dhayaçiraḥ kṛtvā nānāmūrtibhir āvṛtam / antardadhau sa viçveço viveça ca rasāṁ prabhuḥ*). Having arrived there Viṣṇu began in a melodious voice to recite Vedic hymns. The two demons hearing this go to find out the origin of these sweet sounds, neglecting the Veda's. In the mean time Viṣṇu takes the Veda's, and gives them back to Brahmā. The two asura's come back after having sought in vain for the divine singer. Not finding the Veda's, they look for Viṣṇu and challenge him to battle. In his horse-headed shape he defeats them. The story ends with the words: "Thus did the majestuous Hari formerly assume the form with the horse's head. This boon-granting, lordly shape is celebrated as an ancient form of his" (*evam eva mahābhāgo babhūvāçvaçirā hariḥ / paurāṇam etat prakhyātaṁ rūpaṁ varadaṁ aiçvaraṁ*).

Before discussing these motifs further, I must first mention some other places where the name Hayagrīva appears in the epic with another value than as an epitheton of Viṣṇu.

Mah. XII, 24, 23—34 describes how Kṛṣṇa points out to the King Yudhiṣṭhira that he is neglecting his royal duty when he prefers the life of a hermit to royalty. He puts before him the example of the heroic Hayagrīva, a King of olden days, who died on the battlefield, fighting against the superior forces of the enemy. Now he enjoys heavenly bliss.

Just the opposite of this good king is Hayagrīva, the king of the Videha's, who is mentioned in Mah. V, 74, 15. The Pāṇḍava Bhīma here speaks exceptionally gentle words, and mentions the bad example of eighteen kings, who slew their relatives and friends. Among these he also mentions Hayagrīva, king of the Videha's.

These two cases I only cite for the sake of completeness, as I do not dare to draw them into my discussions.

Of direct importance to my subject, however, are demons with the element "horse" contained in their names, which are repeatedly mentioned in enumerations of dānava's. So Mah. I, 65 mentions among the sons of Danu (*dānava's*) next to Çambara, Puloman, Keçin etc. also Açvaçiras, Açvagrīva, Açvaçaṅku, Açva and Açvapati. Is one of these identical with the dānava Hayagrīva, who is mentioned V, 130, 50? Vidura there describes the miraculous power of Kṛṣṇa to Duryodhana, and says among other things: "While sleeping on the vast deep he slew Madhu and Kaiṭabha, and in another birth Hayagrīva too was slain" (*ekārṇave ca svapatā nihatau madhukaiṭabhau / janmāntaram upagamya hayagrīvas tathā hataḥ*). We have seen that Madhu and Kaiṭabha were killed on account of the theft of the Veda's. Was Hayagrīva punished for a similar transgression? This passage gives no further information, and only implies that the slaying of Hayagrīva took place later.

In the Mahābhārata Hayagrīva thus appears in the first place as a special form of Viṣṇu, in which he promulgates the Veda's and defeats two demons who steal them; and in the second place as an asura, who is killed by Viṣṇu at one occasion or another not further described.

In the supplement to the Mahābhārata, the Harivaṁça, we find again the horse-headed form of Viṣṇu mentioned as the slayer of the two demons Madhu and Kaiṭabha, and as the restorer of the Veda's. In Harivaṁça 2928 sq., this incident is depicted in a form slightly differing from of the description in Mah. XII, 347: "Nārāyaṇa and Brahmā, floating on the deep, during many years remained resting on the waters, without moving themselves. Then after a long time Madhu and Kaiṭabha repaired to this place where Brahmā was resting. Then, in those times of yore, Brahmā, having seen the two asura's, horrible, tall and hard to vanquish, struck Viṣṇu with a lotus-stalk. Viṣṇu at once rose from his berth, sending forth a great effulgence. Then a terrible fight took place between the two (asura's) and Viṣṇu, in the world, that then had turned into one ocean, the three worlds having turned into water" (*tāv ubhau jalagarbhasthau nārāyaṇapitāmahau / bahūn varṣagaṇān apsu çayānau na cakampatuḥ / atha dīrghasya kālasya tāv ubhau madhukaiṭabhau / ājagmatus tam uddeçaṁ yatra brahmā vyavasthitaḥ / dṛṣṭvā tāv asurau ghorau mahākāyau durāsadau / brahmaṇā tāḍito viṣṇuḥ padmanālena vai purā / utpapātāçu çayanāt padmanābho mahādyutiḥ/tad yuddham abhavad ghoraṁ tayos tasya ca vai tadā / ekārṇave tadā loke trailokye jalatāṁ gate*). In Har. 15360 sq. we find this motif again summarized, but now the theft of the Veda's is especially recorded: "When formerly two dānava's stole the Veda's from under the very eyes of Brahmā, they were recovered by thee, o God! (i.e. Viṣṇu).... Having assumed the horse-headed form, and having killed Madhu and Kaiṭabha, thou gavest the Veda's back to Brahmā...." (*dānavābhyāṁ hṛtā vedā brahmaṇaḥ paçyataḥ purā / paritrātās tvayā deva....; kṛtvā hayaçirorūpam hatvā tu madhukaiṭabhau / brahmaṇe te 'rpitā vedāḥ....*). When Viṣṇu comes from battle as conqueror he is praised by the muni's, and then takes on a wonderful mystic form, which is described in Har. 11988 in terms which remind one strongly of Mah. XII, 347, where is stated that he takes this form before slaying the Veda-thieves. The description in Har. runs: "Having been praised in this way by the different saints and ascetics, the great Hari remembered and assumed his vast body with the horse's head. The Veda's made up his shape, his body consisted of all the gods; in the middle of his head was Çiva, in his heart was Brahmā; the rays of the sun were his hair, the sun and the moon were his eyes; the Vasu's and Sādhya's were his legs, in all his joints were the gods. Agni was his tongue, the goddess Satyā his speech, while his knees were formed by the Maruts and Varuṇa. Having assumed this form, a great wonder to the gods, he pressed the asura down, with eyes that were red with anger" (*stūyamānaç ca vividhaiḥ siddhair munivarais tathā / sasmāra vipulaṁ dehaṁ harir hayaçiro mahān / kṛtvā vedamayaṁ rūpaṁ sarvadevamayaṃ vapuḥ / çiromadhye mahādevo brahmā tu hṛdayasthitaḥ / ādityā raçmayo vālāç cakṣuṣī çaçibhāskarau / jaṅghe tu vasavaḥ sādhyāḥ sarvasandhiṣu devatāḥ / jihvā vaiçvānaro devaḥ satyā devī sarasvatī / maruto varuṇaç caiva jānudeçe vyavasthitāḥ / evaṁ kṛtvā tathā rūpaṁ surāṇām adbhutaṁ mahat / asuraṁ pīḍayām āsa krodharaktāntalocanaḥ*).

These are the only places in the Harivaṁça where Viṣṇu is described with the horse's head. He is then continually mentioned as Hayaçiras.

The demon Hayagrīva, however, who is only slightly mentioned in Mah. V, 130 as an enemy of Viṣṇu, here on the contrary takes a very prominent position.

From the many passages where he is fully described, one can form a rather clear image of him. In the first place it is striking that in the whole Har., he is always denoted by the epitheton "heroic" (*hayagrīvaç ca vīryavān*, Har. 203, 2281, 2650, 12985; *balavān*, 13380, 14282). In accordance with this he is then nearly always depicted in appreciative terms. In Har. 203 he is mentioned in the enumeration of the dānava's, the sons of Kaçyapa and Danu. Just as in Mah. I, 65 (see above) he is mentioned together with Puloman, Keçin, Çambara etc., but the names Açvaçiras and Açvagrīva are missing here. As the enumeration of dānava's as it is given in the Har. is the oldest one [1]), one may conclude from this fact, that afterwards, when the demon Hayagrīva gained more importance, by his side there were created analogous figures, with the element "horse" in their names.

Now we find repeatedly in the Har. the demon Hayagrīva mentioned as an enemy of the gods, especially of Viṣṇu. So for instance in the description of the different avatāra's of Viṣṇu. In three steps the god measures the universe. Among the dānava's who oppose him is mentioned the "heroic Hayagrīva" (Har. 2281). He also appears in the great Tārakā-battle. The gods are fallen upon by the dānava's, and Viṣṇu comes to their aid. Har. 2433 says then: "The dānava Hayagrīva appears in his chariot, drawn by a thousand horses, crushing the enemies" (*yuktaṁ hayasahasreṇa hayagrīvas tu dānavaḥ / syandanaṁ vāhayām āsa sapatnānīkamardanaṁ*). Elsewhere is related that the mighty dānava Naraka becomes over-bold and offends the gods. He goes to battle with four generals, viz. Hayagrīva, Nisunda, Pañcanāda and Muru. Lines 6867 sq. describe how Hayagrīva bravely fights Viṣṇu: "Then the dānava, his eyes red with anger, runs forward like a stormwind, and, having climbed and rooted up a tree of ten fathoms, he rushes on him (i.e. Viṣṇu) with it. He hurls this enormous tree, that resembles a cloud, with dexterity, and a roaring noise is heard when this tree cleaves the wind. But Viṣṇu without delay sending forth a thousand arrows breaks this tree, as if it were a piece of cucumber, in many pieces. Then with one arrow he pierces the breast of Hayagrīva. The flaming missile enters the middle of his breast, and by its excessive speed, having cleft the heart, it leaves the body. He, the terrible, the strong Hayagrīva who, single-handed, had fought all the gods during a thousand years, was killed by the Invincible One" (*punas tu krodharaktākṣo vāyuvegena dānavaḥ / daçavyāmocchritaṁ vṛkṣaṁ samāruhya vanaspatiṁ / vṛkṣam utpāṭya vegena pragṛhya tam adhāvata / cikṣepa sumahāvṛkṣam çikṣayā tu ghanākṛtiṁ / vṛkṣavegāniloddhūtaḥ çuçruve sumahāsvanaḥ / tataḥ çarasahasreṇa tvaramāṇo janārdanaḥ / tañ ca ciccheda citrabhaktinibhākṛtiṁ / punaç caikena vāṇena hayagrīvasya corasi / vivyādha*

1) Cf. W. Kirfel, Das Purāṇa Pañcalakṣaṇa, Bonn 1927, page XXXIII.

stanayor madhye sāyako jvalanaprabhaḥ / viveça so 'tivegena hṛdi bhittvā vinirgataḥ / yaḥ sahasraṁ samās tv ekaḥ sarvān devān ayodhayat / taṁ jaghāna mahāghoram hayagrīvaṁ mahābalaṁ). But with this Hayagrīva has not yet disappeared from the stage. For the dānava's who were killed in the Tārakā-battle are reborn in the town where Viṣṇu, reincarnated as Kṛṣṇa shall appear on earth. Har. 3109 sq. describes the reincarnation of Hayagrīva: "He that, mettlesome as a horse, was known as Hayagrīva is reborn as the steed Keçin, youngest brother to Kaṁsa. This bad one, loudly neighing, unchecked, with flowing mane, lives alone in the Vṛndā-wood, and eats human flesh" (*yo 'py asau hayavikrānto hayagrīva iti smṛtaḥ / keçī nāma hayo jātaḥ kaṁsasyaiva jaghanyajaḥ / sa duṣṭo heṣitapaṭuḥ keçarī niravagrahaḥ / vṛndāvane vasaty eko nṛṇāṁ māṁsāni bhakṣayan*). When later another description is given of the struggle between gods and demons, Hayagrīva the strong (*balavān*) appears again, accompanied by a multitude of asura's, who, strangely enough, have all horse's heads (*hayagrīvair mahāsuraiḥ*). He is then described as: "resembling a white rock, adorned with white ear-rings, standing in his chariot he shone like a white-topped mountain. On his standard that glitters with beryl, coral and other kinds of gems and precious stones, one sees a seven-headed serpent. Hundreds of asura's of immeasurable strength and great valour, having the best war-chariots, follow him like the gods follow Indra" (Har. line 12989 sq.: *çvetaçailapratikāçaḥ çvetakuṇḍalabhūṣaṇaḥ / çuçubhe rathamadhyasthaḥ çvetaçṛṅga ivācalaḥ / mahatā saptaçīrṣeṇa rājatā nāgaketunā / vaiḍūryamaṇicitreṇa pravālāṅkuraçobhinā / amitabalaparākramadyutīnāṁ vararathinām anujagmur ūrjitānāṁ / asuragaṇaçatāni gacchamānaṁ tridaçagaṇā iva vāsavaṁ prayāntaṁ*). Finally Har. 13380 sq. gives a detailed description of the violent battle between Hayagrīva and Pūṣan, in which the latter is defeated and put to flight.

The incarnation of Hayagrīva as Keçin is clearly a later motif. The Viṣṇu-purāṇa gives the older version of this story; here Keçin is not at all connected with the demon Hayagrīva. He is a demon who has the shape of a horse, sent by Kaṁsa to kill the two children Kṛṣṇa and Rāma. In V, ch. 15 Kaṃsa says: "I will order the fierce Keçin, who haunts the Vṛndā-wood, to attack them, and he is of unequalled might, and will surely kill them" [1]). In ch. 16 is described how Keçin came to Kṛṣṇa: "He came in the shape of a steed, spurning the earth with his hoofs, scattering the clouds with his mane, and springing in his paces beyond the orbits of sun and moon" [2]). But Kṛṣṇa thrusts his arm into the mouth of this monster-horse and causes it to swell slowly, until the horse bursts.

1) Cf. Wilson, The Viṣṇu Purāṇa, London 1840, p. 537.

2) Ibid., page 539.

The fact that Keçin as well as Hayagrīva, by their names and their descriptions suggest a horse's shape, and were considered as adversaries of Viṣṇu, gave rise to the identification by rebirth (a very frequently occurring feature in Indian literature), which is dealt with in the Harivaṁça.

We see the figure of the demon Hayagrīva gradually growing more important; a growth which finds its continuation in the later literature.

With regard to the Viṣṇupurāṇa we have to note that here Viṣṇu is incidentally called the Horse-headed One. Important is V, ch. 17, where the horse is mentioned as an avatāra of god Viṣṇu: [1]) "He, the unborn, who has preserved the world in the various forms of a fish, a tortoise, a boar, a horse, a lion, will this day speak to me". Here the horse takes the place often occupied by Vāmana, the dwarf. The commentary at this passage says that the horse stands here for Hayagrīva, the horse-headed shape of Viṣṇu. This passage is the only one in the old literature, as far as I know, where the Hayagrīva-form of Viṣṇu is positively mentioned in the list of the avatāra's. Probably it is a later interpolation, inserted with many others, when this text became the principal work of the Vaiṣṇava's.

The Purāṇa of the Vaiṣṇava-sect which at the present time is best known, is the Bhāgavata-purāṇa; this book has been composed much later. In VI, 6, 29 we find Hayagrīva mentioned once more as a dānava, one of the sixty sons of Danu. In this list Puloman, Çambara etc. again appear. VI, 10, 19 and VIII, 10, 21 mention him among the asura's, who start fighting with the gods. And when in VII, 2, 4 Hiraṇyakaçipu sees that Viṣṇu in the shape of a wild boar kills his brother, he delivers a wrathful harangue to the assembled dānava's; among them Hayagrīva together with other asura's joins Vṛtra in the battle against Indra, who has armed himself with the bones of Dadhīca [2]).

In this purāṇa the theft of the Veda's is found in VIII, 24, 8, where the fish-avatāra of Viṣṇu is described: "At the end of the former kalpa there was the destruction (of the universe) named after Brahmā. Then, o King, the earth and the other worlds were flooded over by the ocean. When the Creator who was sleepy dozed off for a moment, the strong Hayagrīva robbed the Veda's that had come out of his mouth. The noble Lord Hari, knowing what had been done by Hayagrīva, the King of the dānava's, took on the form of a çapharī-fish" (*āsīd atītakalpānte brāhmo naimittiko layaḥ / samudropaplutās tatra*

1) Ibid., page 541.

2) Endeavours have been made to connect Dadhīca, who also has a horse's head, with the general conception of the horse-headed figure; cf. Bosch, in: Tijdschr. v. N. I. Taal, Land en Volkenk., LXVII, 1927, p. 124.

lokā bhūmyādayo nṛpa / kālenāgatanidrasya dhātuḥ çiçayiṣor balī / mukhato niḥsṛtān vedān hayagrīvo 'ntike 'harat / jñātvā tad dānavendrasya hayagrīvasya ceṣṭitaṁ / dadhāra çapharī-rūpam bhagavān harir īçvaraḥ). Then the story of the deluge is related at greath length; thanks to the warning of the fish, the good King Satyavrata and the seven Ṛṣi's are the only ones who escape. At the conclusion of the episode we find: "When the danger of the destruction was over, Hari, having killed the demon Hayagrīva, brought back the Veda's to the Creator who had arisen from his sleeping position" (*atītapralayāpāya utthitāya sa vedhase / hatvāsuraṁ hayagrīvaṁ vedān pratyāharad dhariḥ*). This same story is related in the Agni-purāṇa.

In Bhāgavata-purāṇa II, 7, 11 Brahmā alludes to the theft of the Veda's with the following words: "In my sacrifice then the noble Horse-headed One [1]) was the Sacrificial Male himself, of golden complexion, full of incantations and sacrifices; whose soul were all the gods, and from whose nostrils sweet words were created when he breathed" (*sattre mamāsa bhagavān haya-çirṣātho / sākṣāt sa yajñapuruṣas tapanīyavarṇaḥ / chandomayo makhamayo 'khiladevatātmā / vāco babhūvur uçatīḥ çvasato 'sya nastaḥ*)..... "And he recovered the trace of the Veda's that had fallen out of my mouth in the terrible waters" (*visraṁsitān urubhaye salile mukhān ma / ādāya tatra vijahāra ha vedamārgān*). Cf. further allusions in VII, 9, 37 and XI, 4, 17.

At this passage the commentator Çrīdhara remarks that Hayaçīrṣan, the Horse-headed One, must be understood as Viṣṇu's descent as the Hayagrīva-avatāra. This is then the last stage in the process of evolution; in the later literature we find this evolution extensively dealt with.

The Devī-bhāgavata-purāṇa for instance relates "that Hayagrīva, having received boons similar to those received by Hiraṇyakaçipu, that he should not be assailable by man or beast, began to give trouble to the gods. The gods thereupon went to the Devī and implored her aid. She directed them to go to Viṣṇu and request him to be born upon earth with the face of a horse and the body of a man, and kill the rākṣasa. The gods prayed to Viṣṇu accordingly; and pleased by their prayer, Viṣṇu became incarnated in a form half-horse and half-man, and hence known as Hayagrīva, and destroyed the rākṣasa Hayagrīva" [2]).

About the year 1700 Nābhadāsa wrote his great work about the Vaiṣṇava-reformation of Rāmānuja (12th century), the Bhaktamālā. It is here that we finally find Hayagrīva positively mentioned in the official list of avatāra's, where he occupies the

1) In X, 6, 22 the shepherdesses invoke Viṣṇu as Hayāsya.

2) Gopinath Rao, Elements of Hindu Iconography, Madras 1914, Vol. I, part I, page 260.

18th place [1]). This fixed position he keeps also in the popular belief. Together with Dattātreya, Mohinī, etc., he is reckoned among the so-called "minor avatāra's" [2]).

Taking now into consideration the total of the material collected, we discover, notwithstanding the great variety, an obvious tendency, viz. the gradual convergence and final amalgamation of two motifs, which are originally totally different; one, the horse-headed shape of Viṣṇu; the other, the demon Hayagrīva, whose name also suggested a horse-headed appearance.

This demon Hayagrīva seems to have played only an unimportant rôle in the beginning. However, by his suggestive name, this figure advances more and more to the front. Then the demon Hayagrīva enters the list against Hayaçiras, god Viṣṇu as a demon-destroyer. The fight between the two is described: this incident is apparently made up in analogy with other stories of demons, who are slain by Viṣṇu, for instance Madhu, Hiraṇyakaçipu etc. As the motive for the slaughter of the demon Hayagrīva the theft of the Veda's is mentioned. Herewith we remain completely in the sphere of the old association: the horse-headed figure and the reciting of the Veda's.

In the mythical world of thought we distinguish in general two contrary tenors. On one side an inclination to diverge and differentiate: one and the same theme is dissected into small subdivisions, which gradually loosen themselves totally from the old connection and develop into independent themes.

On the other hand, however, a converging and assimilating tenor is traceable; two or more themes, which originally have nothing in common, become gradually identified through an incidental conformity, and finally melt together in unity.

In the history of the development of the horse-headed figure we meet with an apparent case of convergence. The final result of this process is one of those paradoxical combinations, much beloved by Indians: Hayagrīva kills Hayagrīva [3]).

---

1) Grierson, Gleanings from the Bhaktamālā, Journal of the Asiatic Society, 1909.

2) Cf. Rao, op. cit., and also: Gravely and Ramachandra, Catalogue of the South Indian Hindu metal images in the Madras Government Museum, Madras 1932, p. 8.

3) It would be interesting to investigate what place should be awarded in this connection to the story which is told in Har. ch. 199 about the slaughter of Madhu and Kaiṭabha. These two demons here voluntarily suffered death by Viṣṇu, and request from him the favour of rebirth as his incarnation. In the first place one must solve the chronological question: from which time would this part of the Har. date? It would also be well worth the trouble to institute a closer inquiry into the background of the Rāmarāmavivāda, the fight between Rāma and Paraçu-rāma, both of them incarnations of Viṣṇu. Perhaps this incident has influenced the motif of "Hayagrīva slaying Hayagrīva".

I have on purpose repeatedly quoted in their entirety those passages in which the Horse-headed figure is fully described. These descriptions must have made an exceptional impression on the later reader and will have contributed to the fact that Viṣṇu in this mystical shape with the Horse's head enjoyed special favour. Finally these descriptive passages, together with the (resultant?) iconographic indications in the different āgama's, must have inspired the plastic artists to the creation of images in bronze and stone.

In the Hindu-literature the Hayagrīva-theme is repeatedly treated by itself, chiefly by authors influenced by Viṣṇuism.

In the first place, the motif of Viṣṇu with the horse's head. To this figure many songs of praise are dedicated. The best known is the Hayagrīvastotra by Veṅkaṭanātha [1]. Moreover one sees this wonderful shape of Viṣṇu appearing in the titles of books, where he by his presence enhances their religious value. I mention as an example the Hayagrīva-upaniṣad [2], the Hayaçīrṣa-pañcarātra [3] etc. In the second place the motif of the demon Hayagrīva and his death at the hands of Viṣṇu. This subject has been treated in a drama Hayagrīva-vadha, "The Death of Hayagrīva", by the poet Bhaṛtrmeṇṭha [4].

Viṣṇu in his horse-headed form has also often been chosen as a subject by plastic artists. The well-known scholar Hemādri (1260—1309 A.D.) cites some instructions as to how Viṣṇu in this form must be represented: "The horse-headed god should be made with his spread feet placed in the hands of the Goddess Earth. He should have a white complexion, and wear blue garments. The god should be made with eight arms; four of these the wise man should make keeping the conch, the discus, the club and the lotus. The four other hands should be placed upon the heads of the four Veda's personified, and the god should be adorned with all the usual ornaments" (*mūrtimān pṛthivīhastanyastapādaḥ sitacchaviḥ / nīlāmbaradharaḥ kāryo devo hayaçirodharaḥ / kartavyo 'ṣṭabhujo devaḥ tatkareṣu catuṣvatha / çaṇkham cakraṁ gadāṁ padmaṁ svākāraṇ kārayed budhaḥ / catvāraç ca karāḥ kāryā vedānāṁ dehadhāriṇām / devena mūrdhni vinyastāḥ sarvābharaṇadhāriṇā*). The Pañcarātra Āgama describes another form, where the god has only four hands; these hold the conch, the rosary, and the book, whilst the fourth shows the *jñāna-mudrā* [5].

---

1) Edited in Vedānta Deçika, Çrīraṅgam 1909.

2) Cf. One Hundred and Eight Upanishads, ed. by Wasudev Laxman, Bombay 1925, page 539.

3) Cf. Eggeling, Cat. India Office, No. 2611.

4) Cf. Rājataranginī, III, 260 sq.: hayagrīvavadhaṁ meṇṭhas tadagre darçayan navaṁ, etc.

5) Cf. Krishna Sastri, South-Indian Images of Gods and Goddesses, Madras 1916, p. 55.

In the Laksmīnarasiṁha-temple at Nuggehalli (Mysore) two beautiful statues have been preserved, representing Viṣṇu-Hayagrīva, with respectively four and eight arms [1]).

The eight-armed figure (see Plate I) is represented *en profile*. The horse-head is clearly visible. The god appears to be performing a dance of triumph on the corpse of his enemy, which lies stretched out upon the ground. He is richly decked out with ornaments, and wears his high kirīṭa-makuṭa crown. In the four right hands he carries the club (*gadā*), arrow (*bāṇa*), discus (*cakra*), and sword (*khaḍga*). In the four left hands: conch (*çaṅkha*), shield (*kheṭaka*), bow (*dhanuṣ*) and lotus (*padma*). This statue is a fine piece of work by the eminent sculptor Mallitamma (13th century); next the signature of this artist, the pedestal of the statue shows an inscription which declares that this is a representation of Hayagrīva.

The second Plate shows Hayagrīva *en face*, with four arms, sitting cross-legged upon a lotus-throne. Here he also wears the kirīṭa-makuṭa on the clearly recognisable horse-head. Unfortunately the objects which he holds in his four hands have been damaged, but they appear to agree with the description of the Pañcarātra Āgama: the one right hand shows, crossed before the breast, the jñāna-mudrā, thumb and middle-finger touching each other. The uplifted right hand shows the rosary (*akṣamālā*).

In popular religion Viṣṇu-Hayagrīva is generally represented in a standing position, with two or four hands. If he has two hands, then he carries in them the conch and the discus [2]). If he is represented with four hands then he carries besides them also a sword and a shield (see Plate III). Conch and discus are here conventionalized in two similar motifs, the one perfectly the same as the other. The development of this similarity is depicted in Gravely, op. cit. page 22—23.

In the later developments of Hinduism the fierce (*bhairava*) gods gain ever more importance.

In the first place Çiva, who has by nature already a very terrible character (*raudra*) in his quality as "all-destructive".

Next him, however, we now see Viṣṇu-Hayagrīva also gradually playing a great part. In my opinion he owes this promotion to the fact that his special mystic form with the horse's head as awe-inspiring demon-exterminator takes such a prominent place in the

1) Cf. Report of the Archaeological Department for the year 1912—13, Mysore, page 2—3.

2) Cf. GRAVELY, op. cit., page 8.

later literature, and, moreover, the fact as well which we mentioned above, that he was so closely connected with the demon Hayagrīva.

On account of these circumstances his figure lent itself particularly to a transformation into a Bhairava-god. At the same time one must keep in mind the fact that the background of the horse-headed figure was formed by the ancient Indian horse-cult, connected with sun and fertility rites. If the later Indians were consciously sensible of this background or not I can not decide; but undoubtedly the existence of this connection, whether consciously or not, has contributed to the fact that Hayagrīva advanced into the foreground; for fertility rites play also a very large part in Çāktism, the veneration of the female energy of Çiva, and his union with her, with the resultant maithuna-rites.

In the later Hindu literature one finds many detailed descriptions of the magical power of Viṣṇu-Hayagrīva. For example, the ninth chapter of the Yoginī-tantra is wholly dedicated to the history and the veneration of the figure of Viṣṇu-Hayagrīva (vulgo: Hayagrīva Mādhava) in the temple on the Maṇikūṭa mountain, near the village of Hajo, Assam [1]). This story is composed in the usual form of a conversation between Çiva and his spouse Pārvatī. Moreover the Kālikā-purāṇa gives in chapter 82 a description of the heroic deeds of Viṣṇu-Hayagrīva, localised in North-India.

This magical aspect of Viṣṇu-Hayagrīva one finds further illustrated in the collections of mantra's (magic formulae) which are specially dedicated to him. The Hayagrīvasahasrākṣaramahāmantra (ms. in Grantha-character, Catalogue India Office, soon to be published, No. 6207) in particular gives a very clear idea of this god in his quality of dispenser of material benefits. See further also the Hayagrīvamahāmantra (ibid., No. 6206), and the Nārāyaṇīyamantrarahasya (ibid., No. 5713).

In the following we shall now see that the later Buddhism wholly dissociates this demonical aspect of Viṣṇu-Hayagrīva from the great Hindu-god, and incorporates him as a special deity in the Mahāyānic pantheon.

2. Hayagrīva in Buddhism

When one begins an inquiry about the horse and the horse-headed figure in Buddhism, then as a matter of course one thinks in the first place of the horse Kaṇṭhaka that carried the Exalted One from the sheltered palace into the world. But after the

---

1) Cf. GAURINATH CHAKRAVARTI, Notes on the Worship of Hayagriba Madhaba by the Hindus and the Buddhists (Journal Buddh. Text Society, Vol. II, 1894, App. II).

I. Hayagrīva, Lakṣmīnarasiṁha Temple. (p. 21)

II. Hayagrīva, Lakṣmīnarasiṁha Temple. (p. 21)

fulfilment of that sacred task, this horse no longer comes to the front in Buddhism.

An important place, however, is taken by the steed Uccaiḥçravas which belongs to the Saptaratnāni, the Seven Treasures of a Cakravartin, a World-ruler, and as such is known by the name Açvaratna. This horse was, together with the other jewels, taken over into Buddhism: for if the Prince Siddhārtha had not turned into the Path to Buddha-hood, then he would have become a World-ruler. This Açvaratna is generally represented as carrier of the Cintāmaṇi, the Wish-granting Jewel. Another aspect of this Açvaratna is the divine horse Balāha, which in Northern Buddhism plays a great part on account of its connection with Avalokiteçvara. The Bodhisattva Avalokiteçvara is one of the most popular gods of the Mahāyānic Pantheon. He presides over the present Kalpa, the Bhadrakalpa, which period lasts from the death of Buddha Çākyamuni until Maitreya will become a Buddha. Avalokiteçvara is in particular considered as a personification of compassion with all suffering creatures who are submerged in the sea of birth and death.

The divine horse Balāha now is the saviour, filled with compassion, who rescues some hundred merchants from the claws of man-eating she-devils. The merchants had sailed out to acquire wealth in foreign countries. They suffered shipwreck, and were stranded on an island where they were received by beautiful women with whom they contracted amorous attachments. In reality these women were man-eating rākṣasī's, who desired to devore their victims. The divine horse, however, appears before the merchants, and offers to take them on his back and bring them again to the inhabited world by flying through space. This rescuing horse is in the older versions of the story (dating from the third century, cf. CHAVANNES, Cinq cents contes et apologues extraits du Tripiṭaka chinois, I, p. 224—226) said to have been an earlier incarnation of Buddha. But later on this horse Balāha is regarded as a special form of the Bs. Avalokiteçvara. In the Karaṇḍavyūha one finds the motif worked out in details, and localised on the island of Ceylon [1]). The merchants are led by a certain Siṁhala, they suffer shipwreck near the island Tāmradvīpa, inhabited by rākṣasī's in the form of beautiful women, with whom they marry, just as in the older versions of the story. One night, however, by means of a magic lamp, Siṁhala learns that he and his comrades have fallen into the hands of man-eating demons, and that he will be put to death the following day. But just at the

1) Cf. for the horse Balāha and allied motifs the clever article by GOLOUBEW, Le cheval Balāha, B.E.F.E.O., part XXVII, 1927, p. 223. See also HUBER, Études de littérature Bouddhique, B.E.F.E.O., part VI, p. 21—22 and page 35—36, and HACKIN, L'Art Tibétain, collection de J. BACOT, Paris 1911, p. 87.

opportune moment a wonderful horse appears, who offers to restore them to their fatherland. The horse, however, imposes the condition (the well known märchen-motif) that, on departing, not one of them must be tempted by the wails of the rākṣasī's to cast one glance behind him. The one who does this will be irrevocably plunged into the sea and become a prey to the rākṣasī's. The merchants accept this condition gratefully, but not one of them is able to keep his promise when he hears the heart-rending lamentations of the women they leave behind. Siṁhala alone remains unshaken, and is safely brought back by the horse. In India he raises a large army, and conquers the island Tāmradvīpa. The inhabitants are converted to Buddhism, and the island is renamed Siṁhaladvīpa, Ceylon. It is recorded at the end of the story that Siṁhala is none other than Buddha himself, and that the horse is a form of the Bs. Avalokiteçvara.

It is with a view to the Chinese material to be treated in the next chapter that I have here discussed the divine horse Balāha. In India there seem to exist no definite indications that the horse-headed figure is identified with the horse Balāha. As we shall shortly see there exists undoubtedly an indirect connection between the Horse-headed One and the Açvaratna: both have the epithet Paramāçva, the "Excellent Horse", and both are considered as forms of the Bs. Avalokiteçvara.

The Indian data regarding the taking over of Viṣṇu-Hayagrīva into Buddhism are extremely scarce, and offer but little historical support. Therefore I may be allowed to quote here already some Chinese sources.

It appears therefrom that the Horse-headed One was at a rather early date incorporated in the Mahāyānic Pantheon.

In the Mahāvairocana-sūtra, which was translated into Chinese in the seventh century, Hayagrīva (*ho-yeh-chieh-li-p'o*) is mentioned in the description of the Great Magic Circle (*maṇḍala*) as a Vidyārāja, who is placed close to the figure of Avalokiteçvara. Further in China in 653 A.D. a work was translated in which a special chapter was dedicated to the worship of the Vidyārāja Hayagrīva, who is here understood as an aspect of Avalokiteçvara. Moreover the celebrated Buddhist missionary Bodhiruci translated about 650 A.D. a text in Chinese, where the Vidyārāja Hayagrīva was connected with Amoghapāça, a special aspect of Avalokiteçvara. On the ground of this information we may then assume that, about 500 A.D., the Northern Buddhists in India venerated Hayagrīva as Vidyārāja, and as an aspect of Avalokiteçvara.

We shall now try to discover why Viṣṇu-Hayagrīva was received as Vidyārāja in the Mahāyāna. Vidyārāja is an abbreviation of Vidyādhara-rāja, King of the Vidyādhara's.

The Vidyādhara's are known in Hinduism as a class of genii living in the air. Their daughters, the Vidyādharī's, are heavenly nymphs [1]).

In chapter I, I discussed already the very old Indian belief in the magic formula, the mantra. Southern as well as Northern Buddhism has taken over and continued the cult of these magic formulae [2]). In the Hīnayāna they were preserved under the name of parittā. The doctrine of the magic word, however, reached its apex in the Mahāyāna. Here a new term was coined for the magic formula, namely dhāraṇī, derived from the root dhṛ, "to hold, to carry". The dhāraṇī is the holder, the carrier of magic power. Next to this term also the word mantra remained in current use in the Mahāyāna. If one will make a distinction between mantra and dhāraṇī, then one can say in general that the dhāraṇī is longer than the mantra. A dhāraṇī, as a rule, is composed of a collection of mantra's.

This same root dhṛ is contained in the word Vidyādhara: they also are carriers (*dhara*) of magical knowledge or magic power (*vidyā*). When the Mantrayānic principles begin to flourish, then the Vidyādhara automatically rise greatly in position. The Kings of the Vidyādhara, the Vidyārāja's, occupy important places in the Mahāyānic pantheon. Suggesting dates for this evolution is a precarious task. It is difficult enough already to trace the origin and development of the Mantrayāna itself. Although, as I pointed out in Chapter I, Mantrayānic ideas already existed in Buddhism from the very beginning, one should like to know when these general conceptions were combined and crystallized to form the tenets of one separate sect, differentiated from the Mahāyāna. Chinese tradition mentions as the patriarchs of the Mantrayāna successively:

1. Vairocana. 2. Vajrasattva. 3. Nāgārjuna. 4. Nāgabodhi.
5. Vajrabodhi. 6. Amoghavajra. 7. Hui Kuo.

The first two of this series are thus gods. Another lists commences with 1. Çubhākarasiṁha and 2. I Hsing. Çubhākarasiṁha [3]) originated from Central India. According to the tradition he was a King of Oḍra, who renounced the world and became a monk. In 716 he arrived at the capital of China, where he translated many Mantrayānic

1) For the Vidyārāja in general cf. PRZYLUSKI, Les Vidyārāja, contribution à l'histoire de la Magie dans les sectes mahāyānistes, B.E.F.E.O., part XXIII, 1923, page 301 sq.

2) Cf. WADDELL, The Dhāraṇī cult in Buddhism, its origin, deified literature and images, in: Ostasiatische Zeitschrift, I, 1912—13, p. 155 sq.

3) Cf. the detailed biography in Sung-kao-seng-ch'uan, ch. 2, and the article Zemmui in Mik., p. 1366.

texts. He worked there together with I Hsing [1]), the famous Chinese priest (683—727), who appears as second in the list.

Nāgārjuna [2]) is the famous Mahāyānic teacher, who flourished about the second century A.D. According to the tradition he was in the Iron Tower in southern India initiated by Vajrasattva. Nāgabodhi is said to have been a pupil of Nāgārjuna. Several endeavours have been made by Buddhist authors to fill up the gap of 500 years that severs Nāgabodhi from Vajrabodhi [3]), who appears next in the list of patriarchs, and consequently should have been his pupil. Vajrabodhi was a son of the Indian King Īçānavarman, and turned to Buddhism at Nālandā, in 680. In 719 he came to China, where he worked in Lo-yang until his death about 740. Mik. p. 2248, s.v. Ryūchi, gives an apt summary of the data on Nāgabodhi, supplied by different Chinese and Tibetan sources. I quote here some Chinese opinions. The Cheng-yüan-hsin-ting-shih-chiao-mu-lu [4]), compiled about 800 A.D., mentions Nāgabodhi as teacher of Vajrabodhi. It is said there (Ts. 2157, p. 875), that from his 28th till his 31st year Vajrabodhi stayed in southern India. There he was during seven years a disciple of Nāgabodhi, who seven hundred years ago had been a pupil of Nāgārjuna (oriental authors place Nāgārjuna in the first century B.C.), who was then miraculously still alive. The same author says in his Piao-chih-chi [5]) (Ts. 2120), Ch. VI, that during some hundreds of years Nāgārjuna transmitted the Mahāyānic Doctrine to the ācārya Nāgabodhi. Nāgabodhi transmitted it to the ācārya Vajrabodhi. Vajrabodhi went to the East, and taught it to Amoghavajra. Amoghavajra afterwards went again to the West, to India, and discussed with Nāgabodhi the Eighteen Gatherings of the Vajraçekharasūtra. All other data concerning Amoghavajra, however, do not mention Nāgabodhi, but Samantabhadra as Amoghavajra's teacher during his second stay in India. Then Nāgabodhi is also mentioned as teacher of Çubhākarasiṁha, who, during his study at Nālandā, was a disciple of Dharmagupta. Some Chinese authors think that this Dharmagupta is identical with Nāgabodhi, but this is denied by others. Finally Nāgabodhi is mentioned as teacher of the famous pilgrim Hsüan Tsang. In the Tz'ŭ-en-chuan (Ts. 2053, written about 650 A.D.

1) Cf. biography in Sung-kao-seng-ch'uan, ch. 5, and art. Ichigyō, in Mik., p. 70.

2) Cf. WALLESER, Life of Nāgārjuna, from Tibetan and Chinese sources, Asia Maior, 1923; id., Lebenszeit des Nāgārjuna, Zeitschrift für Buddh., 1925, p. 237; N. DUTT, Aspects of Mahāyāna Buddhism and its relation to Hīnayāna, London 1930, *passim*.

3) Cf. Sung-kao-seng-chu'an, ch. I, and article Kongōchi in Mik., p. 704.

4) For the Chinese characters and further details see *infra*, page .

5) For complete title see Hob. F. A., p. 122.

by Hui Li) is told that in the great Āmra-wood in the Ceka-land, Hsüan Tsang met with an old priest, who turned out to be Nāgabodhi, the disciple of Nāgārjuna. He was then 800 years old, but looked like a man of thirty.

Regarding the two last patriarchs historical information is at our service. Amoghavajra[1]) was born in 705 on the island of Ceylon, and came together with Vajrabodhi in China, where he died about 770. Hui Kuo[2]) was one of his pupils, who died about 800 at Ch'ang-an.

It will be clear that, from a historical point of view, this list of patriarchs has no value; it shows all the characteristics of a later production. Leaving aside Vairocana and Vajrasattva, one comes to Nāgārjuna, who, as the great apostle of the Mahāyāna, was very well suited for being the first human patriarch. He transmitted the Doctrine to Nāgabodhi, a rather vague personality, but known as his pupil. Now we skip some 500 years, and come to Vajrabodhi. We see, that in the ninth century in China several endeavours were made to cover up this gap by ascribing to Nāgabodhi a life of several centuries, relying on statements like that about Hsüan Tsang's meeting. Finally the three last patriarchs are almost contemporaries. I am inclined to conclude from these facts, that the Chinese Mantrayāna as a separate sect never existed on Indian soil. It seems to have originated in China with the famous translators of Indian texts, in which Mantrayānic principles prevailed. To enhance the religious prestige of the sect, the above-mentioned list was constructed. A vague figure like Nāgabodhi was suited very well for linking up the real founders of the sect, like Vajrabodhi and Amoghavajra, with a famous Mahāyānic priest like Nāgārjuna. Probably the list that mentions Çubhākarasiṁha and I Hsing as first patriarchs was the older one, that represented better historical truth. It was replaced by the other list, which accredited to the Chinese Mantrayāna a venerable age. This does not imply, of course, that in India there did not exist similar sects: later on in Bengal and Tibet several are known, and it is very probable that also before the time of Vajrabodhi and Amoghavajra there were one or more Indian teachers, who taught the Mantrayānic principles, condensed into one separate system. In my opinion, however, there did not exist any direct historical connection between one of these schools and the Chinese Mantrayāna.

The time has not yet come for us, however, to settle these points. We should wait

1) Cf. the lengthy biography in Sung-kao-seng-ch'uan, ch. I, and the article Fukū in Mik., page 1896.

2) Cf. the article Keika in Mik., page 430.

until, one day, the Chinese material has been critically treated: a difficult, but by no means impossible task.

For my present subject, however, it is sufficient that we may assume that in India about 500 A.D., at least the Mantrayānic principles were flourishing. This appears clearly from a text like the Mahāmāyūrīvidyārājñī, that was about 320 A.D. translated into Chinese by a Prince of Kucha, Çrīmitra (cf. Ts. 986, 987).

About this time the figure of Viṣṇu-Hayagrīva was taken over in the Mahāyānic pantheon as a Vidyārāja. We may assume this on the evidence of the occurring of Hayagrīva in the Mahāvairocana-sūtra, mentioned above. No doubt can exist, according to my mind, whether the Horse-headed figure owed this acceptance to the fact that in Hinduism Viṣṇu-Hayagrīva was celebrated as the Reciter of the Veda's, the Promulgator of the Sacred Word. In this quality he was exceedingly suitable for a transformation to Vidyārāja. It is true that also other Hindu gods that were not especially associated with the Sacred Word, for example Çiva, appear in the hosts of the Vidyārāja's. But no one reached such a prominent position as Hayagrīva, who was regarded as most closely connected with Avalokiteçvara, and always retained the horse's head as unfailing characteristic. Further all the Vidyārāja's bear a fierce character. Also in this respect the figure of Viṣṇu-Hayagrīva lent itself excellently for the part of a Vidyārāja; for we saw how extensively in Hindu-literature the awe-inspiring shape of Viṣṇu with the horse's head was described, and how closely this figure was connected with the demon Hayagrīva, the strong. This figure fitted in so well in the Mahāyāna, that soon Hayagrīva was wholly dissociated from Viṣṇu. In enumerations of gods where Viṣṇu is also included, Hayagrīva is separately mentioned. His continually increasing importance is moreover aided by the fact that as the Horse-headed One, he is particularly suited to be conceived as a horse-god, or to be amalgamated with local horse-gods. This last appears to have been the case in Tibet and Mongolia. In Tibet he is known as rta-mgrin (coll. tamdin), the "Horse-necked One". He is one of the Dharmapāla's, "Defenders of the Faith", and an awe-inspiring demon-destroyer, Tibetan: drag-gçed, "Terrible Executioner". He is particularly worshipped by horse-traders. Here also the magic power of neighing is brought to the front. At an exorcism he announces his presence by neighing, and at the sound thereof the demons take to flight [1]). He has the same epitheton of "Excellent Horse", Tib. rta-mchog,

1) Cf. GRÜNWEDEL, page 164, 165, and the literature referred to there; GETTY, page 162 sq.; WADDELL, p. 146.

as the Açvaratna. This Horse-jewel is in Tibet also called rluṅ-rta, the "Aerial Horse". He is the swift messenger between this world and the abode of the gods. As such this horse is the special conductor of prayers and magic formulae [1]); therefore it is represented on special banners, encircled by magic formulae. When these banners are flown in the wind, the divine horse will convey the prayers to the gods. Here one distinctly sees the motif of the winged horse Balāha [2]). In general the presence of the Aerial Horse gives a more intensive power to all sorts of magic formulae, and as such plays a similar rôle as the sunbird Garuḍa (the vāhana of Viṣṇu!)

Przyluski has already pointed out that the development of the Vidyādhara's in Buddhism has been apparently one of the factors that effected the advance into the foreground of these figures in later Hinduism. Perhaps Viṣṇu-Hayagrīva has also to thank his important place in later Hinduism (where, as I mentioned above, as bhairava he stands equal to Çiva) to the fact that he took such a prominent place in Buddhism. It is known that a rich interchange existed between Hinduism and Buddhism, as well in the earlier as in the later periods. A comparatively late example is the case of Hayagrīva Mādhava at Hajo, who, as we saw above, is worshipped by the Hindu's as well as by the Buddhists.

In Buddhist iconography Hayagrīva is represented in different forms. He appears separately, or also as a secondary god. I may permit myself to give here a short summary of the most important of these forms. I have supplemented the Indian data with Tibetan material.

3. Iconographical Survey

A. Hayagrīva as a single god

1. Rāga-Hayagrīva.

This form I call Rāga, because Hayagrīva here bears on his crown the image of Amitābha, the progenitor of the Rāga-kula. The Saptaçatikakalpa gives an

1) Cf. Waddell, The Buddhism of Tibet, London 1934, page 411; Schlagintweit, Buddhism in Tibet, Atlas, plate XVII; the best reproduction of a banner of the Aerial Horse is to be found in Journal of the Buddhist Text Society of India, Vol. II (1894), part I; cf. also Bacot, Décoration Tibétaine, Paris, Pl. 24.

2) Waddell thinks (op. cit., p. 411 sq.), on the contrary, that the rluṅ-rta is of Chinese origin, and that its prototype is the Chin. Dragon-horse, *lung-ma*. He confuses, however, the Chinese unicorn *ch'i-lin* with the *lung-ma*; the reproduction which he gives on page 410 represents the lin, as the Chinese inscription on the top, left, correctly indicates. Cf. my discussion of the *ch'i-lin* in Chapter III, section 2. It is a pity that the second impression of Waddell's fine standard-work has not been revised by a sinologist.

extensive description of the appearance of the god, and of the ritual according to which he should be worshipped. I give here the translation of the whole sādhana, together with the Sanskrit text [1]) and the Tibetan translation [2]).

Hail to Hayagrīva! Knowing the thought that inspires all Buddha's, viz.: "The self-substance of all things is essentially not subject to birth and death", one will then see the eight-topped Sumeru-mountain, adorned with the Seven Jewels. In the midst thereof one sees a palace of a thousand miles square. Having entered there, and having first declared one's attachment to the refuge afforded by the Three Jewels etc., by protecting the Body, Speech and Mind, one may create the Magical Circle of the Sun that fills the Sphere. Having then imagined the syllable haṁ that radiates with effulgence, one may then by saying "Hail to all the Vajra's of Body, Speech and Mind, oṁ āḥ hūṁ", make all the Buddha's and Bodhisattva's that are distributed over the immeasurable worlds of

namo hayagrīvāya. ihādyanutpanne(?)nāvasthitaḥ sarvasvabhāva iti saugatamataṁ viditvā tataḥ sumerupṛṣtham aṣṭāsraṁ saptaratnamayaṁ tanmadhye sahasrayojanapramāṅaṁ masūrakaṁ tatropaviçya ratnatrayaçaraṇagamanādipuraḥsaraṁ kāyavākcittam adhiṣṭhāya tenaivākāçavyāpisūryamaṇḍalam abhinirmāya tenaiva haṁkāraṁ jvaladbhāsvarākāraṁ vicintya tato namaḥ samantakāyavākcittavajrāṇām oṁ āḥ hūṁ ityanena daçadiganantaparyantalokadhātuvyavasthitān sarvabuddhabodhisattvān ānīya jñānakāreṇa praveçya punar dvitīyahaṁkāreṇa

(rgya gar skad du. saptaçatikakalpokta hayagrīva sādhanaṁ. bod skad du. rta mgrin rtog pa bdun brgya pa las gsuṅs paḥi rta mgrin gyi sgrub thabs.) dpal rta mgrin la phyag ḥtshal lo. dṅos po thams cad raṅ bṣin gyis mi gnas pa ṣes pa ni bde bar gçegs pa rnams kyi dgoṅs par rig par byas nas. de nas ri rab yan lag bgryad pa rin po che sna bdun gyi raṅ bṣin la deḥi dbus su dpag tshad stoṅ gi tshad kyi gdan la ñe bar ḥdug ste. dkon mchog gsum la skyabs su ḥgro ba la sogs pa sṅon du ḥgro bas lus daṅ dag daṅ yid byin gyis brlabs la. de yis de bṣin du nam mkhaḥ khyab paḥi ñi maḥi dkyil ḥkhor la mṅon par khyab par sprul nas. de la de bṣin du hūṁ yig ḥbar ba las ḥod zer gyi rnam par bsam ṣiṅ. de nas lus dag yid thams cad rdo rje rnams kyis phyag ḥtshal bas oṁ āḥ hūṁ ṣes pa ḥdis phyogs bcuḥi mthar thug paḥi ḥjig rten

1) Sādh., II, p. 509.

2) OSLO, Rgyud vol. 76, folio 242 verso and 243 recto; P. CORDIER, Catalogue du Fonds Tibétain de la Bibliothèque Nationale, Paris 1915, LXXI, 318.

the ten quarters come. Having made them enter (the magic circle) by the different aspects of J ñ ā n a, by uttering a second time the syllable h a ṃ one may startle the Horse-necked One, and make him also enter (the magic circle). By uttering a third time the syllable h a ṁ one may think this: "I possess the vajra-self-substance of Hayagrīva, who has a red complexion; who is greatly awe-inspiring; who has three eyes, and a reddish-brown beard; who appears terrible, with a protruding belly; whose face is showing the fangs, and who is adorned with a garland of skulls with teeth and lips; whose crown is formed by his braided hair; who bears Amitābha on his head; whose second face is a blue horse's head that is neighing; who with one foot tramples upon the Brahmāṇḍa, and with the other on the end of the world; who is adorned with eight serpents; who has the stature of a dwarf; who wears a tigerskin for garment; who is adorned with all ornaments; who threatens all gods and demons, having the Vajra and the staff in his hands; and

hayaskandharaṁ sañcodyānīya praveçya tṛtīyahaṁkāreṇāhameva hayagrīvavajrasvabhāvātmako 'haṁ raktavarnaṁ mahābhayānakaṁ trinetraṁ kapilaçmaçruraudraṁ bṛhadudaraṁ daṁṣṭrakarālinaṁ dantauṣṭhakapālamālinaṁ jaṭāmukuṭinaṁ amitābhaṣiraskaṁ dvitīyamukhaṁ nīlaṁ hayānanam hīhīkāranādinaṁ brahmāṇḍaçikharākrāntaṁ dvitīyena bhavāgraparyantaṁ aṣṭanāgopetaṁ kharvavāmanākāraṁ vyāghracarmanivasanaṁ sarvālaṅkārabhūṣitaṁ sakaladevāsuraṁ tarjantaṁ gṛhītavajradaṇḍaṁ nānāvarnāçca raçmayaḥ sphuraṇasaṁharaṇapūrvakaṁ vicintayediti. mantrajāpa: oṁ hayagrīva hrīḥ hūṁ phaṭ svāhā . asya bhagavataḥ prabhāvāt

gyi khams na bṣugs paḥi saṅs rgyas daṅ byaṅ chub sems dpaḥ rnams gdan draṅs nas ye çes kyi rnam pas rab tu ṣugs te.slar yaṅ hūṁ yig gñis pas rta mgrin yaṅ dag par bskul ṣiṅ gdan draṅs nas rab tu ṣugs te hūṁ yig gsum pas bdag ñid de bṣin du rta mgrin bṣin du rdo rjeḥi raṅ bṣin gyi bdag can sku mdog dmar po ḥjigs su ruṅ ba sbyan gsum pa.drag po sma ra dmar ser can.gsus pa che ba.sal mche ba gtsigs pa.thod paḥi phreṅ ba can.ral paḥi cod pan can.ḥod dpag tu med pas dbu brgyan pa.sal gñis pa sṅo ṣin ḥjigs su ruṅ paḥi hī hīḥi sgra sgrogs çiṅ.tshaṅs paḥi sgo ṅaḥi rtse mo nas rnam par gnon pa.gñis pas srid pa la sogs paḥi mthar thug pa laḥo. klu brgyad kyis brgyan pa.miḥu thuṅ gi rnam pa can. stag gi pags paḥi çam thabs can. sbrul gyi rgyan gyis brgyan pa. lha daṅ lha ma yin mthaḥ dag la bsdigs par mdsad pa.rdo rje daṅ dbyug pa bsnams ba.rta mgrin las kha dog sna tshogs baḥi ḥod zer spro ba daṅ bsdu ba bsam par byaḥo.sṅags ni oṁ hayagrīva hrīḥ who is sending forth an effulgence of many-coloured rays". The mantra runs: oṁ Haya-grīva hrīḥ hūṁ phaṭ svāhā. Thus is explained in the Saptaçatikakalpa in which way one should obtain, through the power of this Venerable One, the magical powers connected with the Wish-granting Gem, the Holy Jar, the Wish-granting Tree, the Elixir of Immortality, and the methods for prolonging one's life. Further by chanting three hundred thousand times the mantra of this Venerable One, one obtains both realms of a Cakravartin. One will live in the abode of the Vidyādhara's, surrounded by all the heavenly nymphs, and enjoying manifold bliss. One will have Çiva as parasol-bearer, Brahmā as minister, Vemacitra as general, and Hari as doorkeeper. All the gods will be one's servants, and the naked teacher Çaṅkara will expose here his doctrine of all the guṇa's [1]). As long as the Venerable Maitreya has not yet obtained Buddha-hood, so long one will remain

cintāmaṇi bhadraghaṭakalpatarurasarasāyanādīni siddhisādhanāni abhimukhi bhavantītyuktaṁ saptaçatikakalpe. kiṅca bhagavato lakṣatrayajāpāt ubhayacakravartirājyamamukhībhavati. anekabhirapsarobhiḥ parivṛtaḥ puraskṛto vidyādharasthāne bahalasukhamanubhavan eva tiṣṭhati. devendraḥ chattradharo bhavati, brahmāca mantrī, vaimacitrī sainyapatiḥ, hariḥ pratihāraḥ. samastadevā avalaganti. nagnācāryaḥ çaṅkaraḥ samastaguṇān upadarçayati. yāvat bhagavān maitreyo nābhisambudhyati tāvat tiṣṭhati. abhisambuddhe cānuttarāyāṁ samyak-

hūṁ phaṭ svāhā ṣes te.bcom ldan ḥdas ḥdiḥi mthus yid bṣin gyi nor bu daṅ.bum pa bzad po daṅ. dpag bsam gyi çiṅ daṅ. bcud daṅ. bcud kyis len la sogs paḥi dṅos grub rnams bsgrubs bsam don du ḥgyur ro ṣes rtog pa bdun brgya pa las gsuṅs so.cis kyaṅ bcom ldan ḥdas kyi bzlas pa ḥbum phrag gsum byas pas ḥkhor los sgyur ba daṅ rgyal srid gñis mdon du ḥgyur ro.lhaḥi bu mo dpag tu med pahi ḥkhor gyis bskod ṣiṅ rig ḥdsin ma mdun du byas te.de la bde baḥi ḥbras bu nams su myoṅ ṣiṅ gnas so. lhaḥi dbaṅ pos gtugs ḥdsin par ḥgyur ro.tshaṅs paḥi sṅags pa daṅ. thag bzaṅs ris kyi dmag dpon daṅ ḥphrog byed daṅ.so sor ḥphrog byed daṅ.lha rnams mthaḥ dag stobs med par ḥgyur ro.gcer bu paḥi slob dpon bde byed daṅ mthaḥ dag gi yon tan rnams ñe bar ston par byed do.ji srid

1) This passage is a sneer at Hinduism. Vemacitra is the King of Asura's. Çaṅkara is the famous Vedānta-philosopher of the 8th century. He originated from the Dekhan, where the Digambara-sect of the Jaina's flourished; probably for this reason he is called here mockingly "naked", the Buddhist author confusing him with the Digambara's. Moreover he wrongly ascribes the doctrine of the three guṇa's, which belongs to Sāṁkhya-philosophy, to the Vedānta-system.

III. Hayagrīva, popular image. (p. 21)

IV. Hayagrīva embracing his çakti. (Getty, Pl. XLIV, c). (p. 37)

(here in this paradise). And when (Maitreya) has become a Buddha, he will predict [1]) to the practitioner that he also shall reach the Highest Enlightenment. The sādhana as it is quoted in the Saptaçatikakalpa is finished.

sambodhau vyākarotīti. saptaçatikakalpoktam hayagrīvasādhanaṁ samāptaṁ.

bcom ldan ḥdas kyis byams pa mṅon par ma rtogs pa de srid du gnas so. mṅon par rtogs nas bla na med pa yaṅ dag par rdsogs paḥi byaṅ chub tu luṅ ston par ḥgyur ro. rtog pa bdun brgya pa las gsuṅs paḥi rta mgrin gyi sgrub thabs rdsogs so.

2. Dveṣa-Hayagrīva.

This form I call Dveṣa, because here Hayagrīva bears on his crest the image of Akṣobhya, the progenitor of the Dveṣa-kula. Again I give the translation of the whole sādhana, side by side with the Sanskrit text and Tibetan translation [2]).

The noble Hayagrīva, obtained according to the ritual described above, by the inspection of the red syllable hūṁ in the sun on the full-blown lotus, should be imagined as having a red complexion; having three faces and eight arms; each face having three eyes; his right face is blue, his left face is white; he is adorned with serpents; his feet are placed in the Lalitakṣepa-attitude; he is looking with angry eyes; his middle face is smiling, his right face shows a rolling tongue, whilst his left face shows the fangs gnawing

purvoktavidhānena viçvakamalasūrye raktahūṁkārajñānaniṣpannam āryahayagrīvaṁ raktavarṇaṁ trimukhaṁ aṣṭabhujam pratimukhaṁ trinetraṁ nīlasitadakṣiṇetaravadanaṁ sarpābharaṇam lalitākṣepapadanyāsaṁ sakrodhadṛṣṭinirīkṣamānaṁ prathamamukhaṁ smeraṁ

(rgya gar skad du. hayagrīva sādhanaṁ. bod skad du. rta mgrin gyi sgrub paḥi thabs. dpal rta mgrin la phyag ḥtshal lo.) sṅon du bstan paḥi cho gas sna tshogs padma daṅ ñi ma la hūṁ dmar poḥi ye çes las yoṅs su rdsogs paḥi ḥphags pa rta mgrin mdog dmar ba. ṣal gsum pa. phyag brgyad pa. ṣal so so nas sbyan gsum gsum mo. sṅon po daṅ dkar po ni gyas daṅ cig ços kyi ṣal lo. sbrul gyi rgyan can. ḥgyin bag gis gnon ciṅ gnas pa khro boḥi lta staṅs kyis gzigs pa. ṣal daṅ po bṣad pa. gyas paḥi

1) Vyākaroti in its technical Buddhist sense.

2) Cf. Sādh., II, p. 508; P. Cordier, Catalogue, LXXI, 85.

the lips; he wears a tiger-skin for garment; his four right hands show the Vajra, the staff, the karaṇa-mudrā [1]), and the arrow, while of his four left hands one is showing the threatening fore finger, and the other is touching his own breast; the remaining two hold the lotus and the bow; he wears the image of Akṣobhya in his crown. This is the meditation called Paramāçvavajra, the Vajra of the Excellent Horse. The mantra runs: oṁ haṁ hayagrīva svāhā. (The Tib. adds: The sādhana of Hayagrīva is finished. It has been made by the paṇḍita Amoghavajra, and it was translated by a bhikṣu-interpreter of Khams).

lalajjihvaṁ dakṣiṇamukhaṁ daṁstrāvaṣṭabdhauṣṭham vāmamukham vyāghracarmanivasanaṁ vajradaṇḍakaraṇamudrāçarodyatadakṣiṇakaracatuṣṭayaṁ tarjanikāsvakucagrahapadmadhanur-udyatavāmakaracatuṣṭayaṁ akṣobhyamaulinaṁ dhyāyāditi. paramāçvavajro nāma samādhi. mantrajāpa: oṁ haṁ hayagrīva svāhā.

ṣal ljags ḥdril ba.mche ba gñis kyis ma mchu btsir ba.gyon paḥi ṣal lo. stag gi pags paḥi çam thabs can no.rdo rje daṅ dbyug pa daṅ.byed paḥi phyag rgya daṅ.mdaḥ ḥphyar ba ni gyas paḥi phyag bṣinḥo.sdigs mdsub daṅ raṅ gi nu ma bzuṅ pa daṅ.padma daṅ gṣu ḥphyar pa ni gyon gyi phyag bṣinḥo.mi bskyod pas mnan paḥi dbu rgyan can bsam par byaḥo ṣes bya ba ni rta mchog ye çes rdo rje ṣes b.ya baḥi tiṅ ge ḥdsin to.sṅags kyi bzlas pa ni.oṁ hayagrīva svāhā. rta mgrin gyi sgrub thabs rdsogs so. paṇḍit don yod rdo rje daṅ khams pa lo tsā va dge sloṅ bris bsgyur baḥo.

3. Paramāçva-Hayagrīva.

In this form Hayagrīva bears the special name of "Excellent Horse". See Bhat., plate XXXIX, d. This picture, drawn by a contemporary Nepalese artist, agrees for the greater part with the sādhana (cf. Sādh., page 510). He has three faces and eight arms. The right face is composed of the fourfold head of Brahmā. The god wears on his own head a large horse-head of a greenish (*harita*) colour. The upper right hand carries the quadruple vajra, the next shows the tripatāka-mudrā (little finger and thumb touching each

1) Bhat., page 193: "Any hand showing this mudrā is outstretched with the index and the little fingers erect, while the thumb presses the two remaining fingers against the palm of the hand". The Tibetan equivalent is explained in the Dictionary of S. C. Das as: "a gesture made in practising magic, in conjuring up or exorcising ghosts".

V. Hayagrīva with the staff; Tibetan thangka painting, 19th century (p. 35)
Collection of the Rijksmuseum voor Volkenkunde, Leiden, The Netherlands, accession number 1383-2. Copyright © Rijksmuseum voor Volkenkunde, 2005.

IX. Hayagrīva of Tjandi Djago. (Brandes, Tj. Djago, Den Haag 1904). (p. 39)

other, the remaining three fingers being erected straight). The two other right hands carry sword and arrow. The four left hands carry the lotus-flower, three peacock-feathers, the staff and the bell. Round his waist he carries a tiger-skin, and he is trampling upon Hindu-gods (cf. BHAT., page 147).

4. Dancing-Hayagrīva.

Another form drawn by a Nepalese artist is shown in BHAT., plate XXV, d. Here Hayagrīva is represented in a dancing attitude, with three heads and eight arms. From his hair a horse's head emerges. Two of the right hands carry the arrow and the mace, whilst a third hand shows the karaṇa-mudrā. His two upper left hands carry the bow and the lotus-flower, whilst the third shows the krodha-muṣṭi (cf. description *infra*, page 53). The two remaining hands are bent to the breast; the right one is carrying the vajra, the left one the noose. He is clad in a tiger-skin.

5. Hayagrīva-Avalokiteçvara.

The god is here represented in his benign aspect, having one head and four hands (cf. BHAT., plate XLIII, 1). The two upper hands carry the rosary and the lotus-flower, the others are bent before the breast, forming the dharmacakra-mudrā. The god sits cross-legged on a lotus seat. The original is to be found in the Macchandar Vahal, at Kathmandu, Nepal. The pictures of the different aspects of Avalokiteçvara there are about twohundred years old.

6. Hayagrīva with the staff.

In this form the god has only one head, and two arms. The right hand carries the staff, raised in a threatening attitude. The left hand, bent to the breast, holds the noose. The colour of the body is red, and from the hair emerges a green horse's head. He wears the tiger-skin, and is adorned with a garland of human heads, and a green snake. Under each foot he crushes an evil spirit. This seems to be his usual appearance when represented in Tibet as tutelary god, Tib. *yi dam* (see Pl. V). A variant with four arms is given in Grünwedel, page 163. There he carries in the upper right hand the vajra-staff, while the other right hand is showing the threatening mudrā. His left upper hand is holding the lotus-flower, the other, bent to the breast, carries the wheel.

7. Hayagrīva with the Iron Sword (*rta mgrin lcags ral can*).

He has one face, and two arms (see Plate VI). On his crown of human skulls he wears a horse's head. His right hand, raised in a threatening attitude, bears a sword. His left hand, bent against the breast, holds the noose. Round the waist he wears a tiger-skin.

VI. Hayagrīva with the Iron Sword (Oldenburg, Sbornik 300 Burchanov, Bibliotheca Buddhica V).

8. The Mysterious Hayagrīva. (*rta mgrin gzaṅ sgrub.*

This is the fiercest form of the god. He has three faces, six arms and eight feet (see Plate VII). His crown is adorned with three horse's heads. His three right hands carry the vajra, the trident, and the sword; his three left hands carry a flame, a banner, and the noose. Round his shoulders he wears a human hide, while the nether part of his body is covered by a tiger-skin. With all his feet he is trampling upon snakes. Cf. also Getty, the bronze statue on Pl. XLIV, *b*; all ornaments of the hands, except the vajra and the grip of the sword, have been lost.

Here it would also seem that might be classed the beautiful small Javanese bronze of Hayagrīva, described by Krom, in "Bijdragen tot Taal- Land- en Volkenkunde van Ned. Indië", part 67, p. 383. The attributes, however, are different, and the figure bears but one horse-head on his crown.

On Tibetan pictures Hayagrīva occurs in this fierce form often as attendant of the Five Dreadful Kings, Tib. Sku lṅa. Cf. the picture 1/1478 in the Leyden Museum.

VII. Mysterious Hayagrīva. (Oldenburg, ibid.)

9. Hayagrīva as summoned by Atīça (*jo boḥi lugs kyi rta mgrin*).

He has three faces and four arms. His crown is adorned with the horse's head (see plate VIII). His upper right hand is carrying the vajra, his upper left hand holds a lotus-flower. The two remaining hands are drawing the bow with an arrow on it. Round his waist he wears the tiger-skin. With each foot he tramples upon an evil spirit. It is said that the god appeared in this form when he was summoned by the famous paṇḍit Atīça (982—1055).

10. Hayagrīva embracing his Çakti.

The çakti is said to be Vajravārāhī or Mārīcī, the goddess of the dawn. As such she too is connected with the sun, and usually represented as standing on a chariot, drawn by seven horses. In the Padma Thang Yig Hayagrīva vanquishes together with her the terrible Rudra (cf. Le Dict de Padma, Padma Thang Yig, transl. by G. C. Toussaint, Paris 1933, p. 39). Her colour, however, is stated to be yellow or red, whilst the çakti of Hayagrīva is always represented as having a blue colour. This question needs further investigation.

VIII. Hayagrīva as summoned by Atīça.
(Oldenburg, ibid.)

The bronze statue in Getty, Pl. XLIV, *c* (see plate IV) has three faces and six hands. The two upper right hands carry the axe and the magic dagger, the two upper left hands hold the sword and the magic staff (khaṭvāṅga). The two remaining hands encircle the çakti, while the left hand is holding a skull-cup (*kapāla*, Tib. thod pa). The god is richly adorned with garlands of skulls, and surrounded by a halo of flames. He is provided with two large wings, which indicate that this statue belongs to the rñiṅ-ma-sect (cf. de Roerich, Tibetan Paintings, Paris 1925, page 37). In this form the god may also carry the quadruple vajra, the sceptre, the vajra and the skull-cup (cf. de Roerich, op. cit. page 39; cf. also the maṇḍala, Leyden Museum, 2286/1).

11. Hayagrīva as the Magic Dagger.

A special aspect of Hayagrīva is his appearance in the shape of the Magic Dagger, S. *kīla*, Tib. *phur bu*. As this form, however, is confined to Lamaism, I need not treat it here. Cf. Getty, Plate LI, where bronze daggers are given; originally they should be made of the demon-deterring Khadira-wood (*acacia catechu*), cf. the specimen of Leyden Museum, 1119/37). For its meaning cf. S. C. DAS, A short description of the Phur-pa, in Buddh. Text Society of India, Vol. IV (1896), part II [1]).

---

1) This form of Hayagrīva is especially interesting because of its ornamentation, which closely resembles that of the Javanese kris. The typical ornamentation of the mystic dagger is as follows. The hilt is formed by a more or less conventionalized vajra; the pommel represents a bhairava-head, usually that of Hayagrīva, characterized by one or three horse's heads on his crest. In some cases the pommel shows a garuḍa-bird. The trilateral blade is topped by a makara-head, from whose yawning mouth it, as it were, comes forth. The blade is decorated by one or two twisted serpents, that sometimes merge into the tongue or the hair of the makara-head. Figure a. shows a bronze magic dagger (drawn after the original in Koloniaal Instituut, Amsterdam, Volkenkundig Museum, No. N. A. M. 29/8), where these motifs may be clearly distinguished. The pommel is formed by the three heads of Hayagrīva, with one horse's head on the crest. It should be noticed how exactly this representation agrees with the directions of the sādhana's: the three eyes and the protruding canine teeth are clearly visible, whilst the left face is showing the rolling tongue. The hilt is formed by the vajra, surmounted by and resting on coiled serpents. Then the makara-head, with the typical curled upper lip, which resembles the trunk of an elephant. The sharp canine tooth and the undulating tongue are noticeable. At the back of the blade one sees *en profile* two entwined serpents.

Figure a

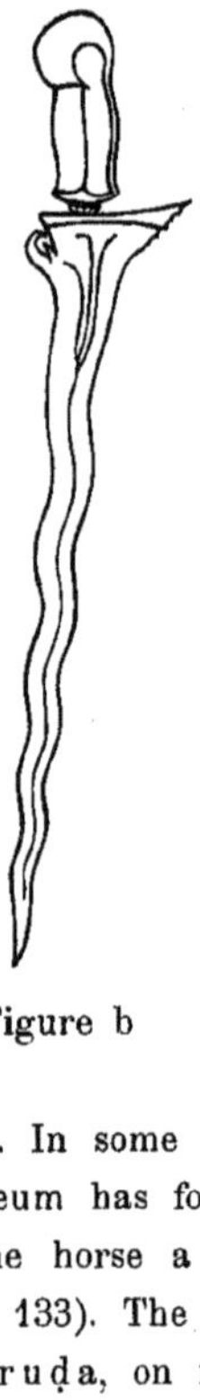

Figure b

The Javanese kris shows this same ornamentation. The blade, straight or undulating, represents a serpent, while the hilt is formed by a conventionalized garuḍa-bird, or by the figure of a demon (buta). The upper edge of the blade, gandja (cf. figure b) shows a curious ornament, the technical name of which is lambé liman, elephant's lip. In this motif we recognize the remnant of a makara-head. Sometimes this lambé liman coincides with the mouth of the serpent, whose body is depicted on the blade (Leyden Museum, Catalogus, Part XI, Java, 1916, Plate IX, fig. 1). In some specimens the analogy with the Tibetan dagger is complete. So kris 1679/6 of the Leyden Museum has for hilt a finely carved horse's head, rising from flower- and leaf-ornaments. On the breast of the horse a standing garuḍa with outspread wings is represented (cf. the drawing in Catalogus XI, p. 133). The idea is worked out further on number 1503/4: the ivory hilt shows a conventionalized garuḍa, on its breast a winged horse is depicted, on its back the sun-disc with twelve rays. These examples prove that the garuḍa as hilt of the kris was conceived as sun-bird, the kuda sembrani of Javanese mythology. So we see that one and the same Indian conception underlies the ornamentation of the Tib. magic dagger as well as the Javanese kris. The typical form of the kris, however, can not be explained from Indian data. Perhaps Takahashi Genji is right when he connects the kris with the ancient Chinese Chou-halberds, which show the same typical shape; similar specimens have been excavated in Japan (Takahashi Genji, Dōboko dōken no kenkyū, Tōkyō 1925). Be this as it may, at any rate our comparison of dagger and kris supplies us with an important suggestion as to the method that should be followed in investigating the Javanese kris: the problem of the ornamentation (Indian), and the problem of the shape (Indonesian, probably connected with China) should be kept strictly apart.

B. Hayagrīva as a secondary God.

As secondary god Hayagrīva as a rule does not bear the horse's head on his crest. Usually, however, he may be recognized by his fierce appearance, his protruding belly, and his snake-ornaments. His attributes are the staff or the club. On paintings his red colour and his tiger-skin are noticeable.

Most frequently he appears together with Tārā, Sudhanakumāra and Bhṛkuṭī in the suite of Avalokiteçvara in his different aspects.

This group of four are the fixed attendants of Amoghapāça Avalokiteçvara. To the left of the central figure Amoghapāça, are Hayagrīva and Bhṛkutī, to the right first Sudhanakumāra and then Tārā. This representation was very popular in Mahāyāna Buddhism, and spread from Northern India all over Tibet, China and the Indonesian Archipelago. In a specimen of this group, found some years ago at Nālandā, Hayagrīva is represented resting with his left hand on the club, while his right hand is raised in greeting. (Cf. photo No. C.C. 2722, Arch. Survey of India; cf. also the photo in FOUCHER, I, p. 101).

In the tjandi Djago (near Tumpang, Java), where in 1268 the ashes of King Viṣṇuvardhana were deposited, a similar group occurred (cf. BRANDES, Tjandi Djago, Den Haag 1904). The stone figure of Hayagrīva of this group (now in the Batavia Museum) is a fine specimen of Hindu-Javanese art (see Plate IX). Body and head are adorned with snake-ornaments. His left hand is resting on the club, the right hand is raised in greeting. The son of Viṣṇuvardhana, the famous King Kṛtanagara, had five bronze copies made of this group.

With this Javanese group may be compared the Nepalese picture (1943 No. 3) in the Leyden Museum, where Amoghapāça is represented with on his left hand first the red Hayagrīva, and next to him Bhṛkuṭī, while at the right hand of the central figure Sudhanakumāra and the green Tārā appear. Hayagrīva wears here on his crown a green horse's head. On Tibetan paintings too this combination is often met with. Cf. for instance GRÜNWEDEL, the reproduction on page 129.

Later on this group of five is extended to far more complicated maṇḍala-like compositions. Then Hayagrīva leaves his fixed place on the left side of the central figure, and is to be found among the bhairava's on the foreground (cf. Leyden Museum, 2285/1).

From the 11th—12th century dates a finely executed dark basalt statue of Avalokiteçvara, with at his left side a smaller image, undoubtedly correctly identified by COHN-as representing Hayagrīva. He may be recognized by his fierce appearance and his raised right hand. Here, however, he appears resting with his left hand on an axe instead of on a club or mace (cf. W. COHN, Asiatische Plastik, Sammlung Bar. E. VON DER HEYDT, Berlin 1932, p. 122; detail-photo of Hayagrīva on page 125).

Further Hayagrīva appears, together with Bhṛkutī etc., as attendant of other aspects of Avalokiteçvara; for instance Khasarpaṇa (BHAT. p. 37, SĀDH. p. 37, 40, 41, 44, 49, 59, 64) and Padmanarteçvara (BHAT. p. 42, SĀDH. page 77).

These are the main places, where Hayagrīva appears as a secondary figure. I may add that occasionally he is represented in his quality of God of Fever on a statue of Parṇaçavarī, together with Çītalā, the Goddess of Small-pox (BHAT., p. 110).

For further representations of Hayagrīva as a minor god see the above-mentioned standard-works of BHATTACHARYYA, FOUCHER, indices s. v. Hayagrīva.

CHAPTER III

HAYAGRĪVA IN CHINA

1. Horse-cult before the introduction of Buddhism

Recent investigations have disclosed that in ancient China fertility and fecundity rites played an important rôle [1]). It is difficult to say with certainty whether the horse was included in those rites. There are, however, some symptoms which point emphatically to this direction. I will try now to follow some of these traces, which lead us back to a remote antiquity.

A reliable description [2]) of the customs and rites that were in vogue during the Chou-dynasty (1050—256 B.C.) may be found in the Chou-li 周禮. In part IV we come across some short records of sacrifices to horse-gods. In the passage where the duties of the equerry, hsiao-jen 校人 are described, we read: "In spring he sacrificed to the Ancestor of Horses.... In summer he sacrificed to the First Horse-breeder.... In autumn he sacrificed to the First Horse-rider.... In winter he sacrificed to the god who looks over the condition of the horses", 春祭馬祖...夏祭先牧...秋祭馬社...冬祭馬步. The commentaries furnish some sparse information about these figures. The Ancestor of Horses is identified as the constellation Fang (Fang-su 房宿, forming part of Scorpio) which also bears the name of Heavenly Horse, t'ien-ma 天馬, or Heavenly four-in-hand team, t'ien-ssŭ 天駟. The commentator Kuo P'o (郭璞, 276—324 A.D.) explains this denomination as follows: "The Dragon is the Heavenly Horse, therefore the four stars named Fang (that form the belly of the Dragon) were called the Heavenly Four-in-hand team", 龍爲天馬、故房四星、謂之天駟. Whereas then in spring this constellation is "en chaleur" sacrifices made in this season are supposed to conduce the fecundity of the horse.

However, it appears to me that this is a secondary explanation. It would be more

---

1) Karlgren, Some Fecundity Symbols in Ancient China (Museum of Far Eastern Antiquities, Bull. 2, Stockholm 1930); Kuo Mo-jo, Researches on Inscriptions on Bones, 郭沫若, 甲骨文字研究, Shanghai 1930.

2) Cf. Karlgren, The early history of the Chou-li and Tso-chuan Texts (Mus. of Far Eastern Antiquities, Bull. 3, Stockholm 1931).

obvious to associate this sacrifice with the horses pulling along the Chariot of the Sun. It is evidenced by several literary records that the ancient Chinese knew of such a conception. The old Sun-hymn Tung Chün 東君, for instance, when speaking of the Sun says: "I drive on my horses" 撫余馬兮. The philosopher Ch'uang-tzŭ (莊子, fourth century B.C.) speaks in Chapter 24 of "ascending the chariot of the sun", 乘日之車. This very antique conception is soon overgrown by other ideas. A later commentary, for instance, says that the horses of the sun are Dragons.

It seems very probable to me that the figure of the Ancestor of Horses is to be associated with these horses of the sun-chariot; this would also be an explanation of the circumstance that spring was selected as the season for sacrificing to this god.

The First Horse-breeder and the First Horse-rider are a couple out of those many anthropomorphic "First Cultivators" in which Chinese mythology abounds.

About the fourth figure nothing in particular is known. The commentary only mentions him as a god who bears malice to horses. I have made an attempt to parallel this name with expressions like t'ien-pu 天步, "the way of Heaven" (cf. Shih-ching II, 8, V2) and kuo-pu 國步, "the fate of the land" (cf. Shih-ching, III, 3, III2), and consequently translated the name as "God that looks over the condition of the horses".

These data, however, are too sparse to produce a firm ground for further conclusions; they only prove the existence of a horse-cult. How the later Chinese tradition supplemented these data will be dealt with in the second part of this chapter.

The horse is furthermore specially mentioned among the gifts that accompany the dead into the grave. The Chou-li (IV, sub ta-ssŭ-ma 大司馬) mentions among the duties of the Great Marshall, ta-ssŭ-ma; "At the funeral sacrifice he should present horses as victims, and announce their arrival to the deceased", 喪祭奉詔馬牲. According to the commentary this ceremony bears the special name of chien-tien 遣奠, the horses are led to the grave; there the Great Marshall solemnly announces their arrival and then the horses are buried together with the deceased (鄭康成曰王喪之以馬祭者、蓋遣奠也。送之至墓、告而藏之). The Equerry performs the work of minor importance in this ceremony: he adorns the horses (here they appear to be the horses of the chariots), and buries them (校人大喪飾遣車之馬、及葬埋之).

Thus we find here a description of the solemn presentation of horses with full ceremonial at the funeral of the King.

Not only the King was given horses along with him into the grave, but also for the grandees and the subjects in general this custom was in vogue. Compare for instance I-LI 儀禮, chapter XIII, Chi-hsi 旣夕. And then we may further quote Ch'un-ch'iu 春秋, under the Duke Yin (隱公, 722—712 B.C.): "In autumn, the seventh month, the King sent the Minister Hsüan to present carriages and horses for the funerals of Duke Hui and his wife Chung-tzŭ", 秋、七月、天王使宰咺來歸惠公仲子賵. The character feng 賵 has the special meaning of the presenting of horses, eventually chariots and horses, at a funeral ceremony. Further particulars regarding this custom are to be found in the LI-CHI 禮記, the Book of Rites. Here we find two kinds of gifts at funeral ceremonies, with different aims, kept strictly apart, viz. in the first place feng, the offering of presents to the deceased, being gifts destined to be buried together with the deceased. And secondly fu 賻, which means: presents given to the relations of the deceased, to defray the expenses of the funeral ceremony. These presents consisted of silk, valuables etc. As a rule feng and fu are mentioned together. So for instance in Li-chi VI, 2, 7, where the good reign of King Wen (Wen Wang 文王) is described; there we read: "As to feng, fu and the precious stones to be put in the mouth of the deceased, they were all submitted to fixed rules", 至於賵賻承含、皆有正法. And in Li-chi VI, 2, 14, where the behaviour of the prince's relations is praised: "They took part in the mourning, and offered fu and feng", 敬弔臨賻賵.

The meaning of the presents that were given to accompany the deceased into the grave was mainly a magical one; they were supposed to communicate magic vitality (yang 陽) to the deceased. This was especially the case with the jade (yü 玉), this being considered as a receptacle *par excellence* of yang-force (cf. KARLGREN, op. cit. page 39). A similar rôle was played by the cowry, pei 貝, in its quality of old fecundity symbol (cf. KARLGREN, op. cit., page 40, and ANDERSSON, Children of the Yellow Earth, London 1934, Ch. XIX, "Aphrodite's Symbol").

Besides these gifts, however, there were others, like utensils and weapons; these were simply meant to accompany the deceased to the Hereafter, and generally they were not supposed to have a special magic power to impart vitality to the deceased.

Now the question is forced upon us: what was the function of these horses, which accompanied the deceased in the grave? Were they supposed to communicate magic force to the deceased, or were they only meant to serve him as draught-horses for his chariots in his life after death?

It seems that the character feng may provide a clue to this question. The ancient form of this character is : thus even in the oldest form of this character, the cowry is already inherent [1]). The character fu on the contrary obtained the radical pei only afterwards [2]); originally it meant nothing more than "to give, to present" generally. Thus the radical pei in the character feng must be interpreted quite differently from the radical pei in the character fu. In fu it was added later to indicate that objects of value were presented. In ancient China the cowry was a usual means of payment; therefore fu is exclusively a contribution to the expenses of the funeral. This appears clearly from passages like Li-chi I, first part, IV, 37; II, first part, II, 34 and XXIX, 47.

Feng on the contrary had a much deeper religious meaning. This is evidenced by Li-chi XV, 6, where horses are also mentioned among fu-gifts, but quite apart from the feng-horses: "The horses that were given to the deceased were led into the ancestral temple; the horses and other presents .... that were given to defray the expenses of the funeral, were not led into the ancestral temple" (賵馬入廟門、賻馬與其幣...不入廟門). Considering this special religious meaning of feng, we may assume that in this character, where from the beginning the element pei was inherent, this pei, the cowry, must be understood in its oldest, original meaning of fecundity symbol. Therefore in my opinion these feng-horses were meant to be magic gifts, for communicating yang-force to the deceased, just like the jade etc.

This would imply that also in ancient China the horse was considered as a fecundity symbol; this fact might be explained from the above-mentioned conception of the horse as combined with the sun.

Such a conception agrees well with the combination sun — sunhorse — fecundity-symbol, that is spread the whole world over (cf. Ch. I).

However other possibilities exist. The material is inadequate to prove that my explanation is right; we may just call it a probability.

2. The Buddhist Hayagrīva

Although one thus may find in ancient China some traces of a horse-cult that was connected with fecundity- and fertility-rites, in the first century A.D., when Buddhism was introduced, it seems that this association had fallen into oblivion. When later on the preachers of the Mahāyāna brought the figure of Hayagrīva to China, there is hardly one tradition with which this Horse-headed One can be linked up.

1) Cf. Takada 高田, Kochū-hen 古籀篇, Tōkyō 1925, vol. 99, page 16, and for this special shape of the cowry vol. 99, page 4.

2) Takada, op. cit., vol. 31, p. 43.

There may exist some connections between the White Horse that according to the later tradition accompanies Buddhist pilgrims to carry the Sacred Books [1]), and the Açvaratna, that is usually represented carrying the Seven or Five-fold Wish-granting Gem. But this motif is sooner connected with Taoist and Confucianist elements than with the special figure of the Horse-headed One. Compare for instance the Hsi-yu-chi 西遊記, composed during the Yüan-dynasty, the fantastic account of the travels of Hsüan Tsang 玄奘, the famous Buddhist pilgrim; here (chapter XV) the White Horse is explained as a transformation of a dragon, who by performing the holy task of the transport of the Sacred Books, expiated a former sin [2]). Perhaps this motif has been influenced by the very ancient Chinese Lung-ma, Dragon-Horse, that in mythical times is said to have emerged from the Yellow River, carrying on its back a mystic map [3]). In this connection one should, in my opinion, explain also the evolution of the Confucian conception of the Unicorn and the Book. Usually the unicorn is represented in plastic arts as holding some books in its mouth, or as carrying them on its back. It is said that before Confucius was born, his mother saw an unicorn appear, that held in its mouth a jade tablet, on which a prophecy regarding Confucius' future glory was written. This is told in the Shih-i-chi 拾遺記, a collection of fabulous tales compiled by Wang Chia 王嘉 (fourth century A.D.). The well-known quotation is lin t'u yü shu 麟吐玉書, "the unicorn spat out the jade writing". By amalgamation with the idea of the White Horse that carries the Sacred Books, this jade tablet was first understood as meaning a real book, and finally by further anology the unicorn was made to carry it on its back.

The ch'i-lin is a very complicated figure; the various elements that have contributed to its present shape have not yet been satisfactorily analysed [4]). It would be of interest, for instance, to investigate whether the often quoted lines: "The feet of the lin do not tread on living plants, they do not crush living insects: this illustrates the virtuous and generous nature of the lin" (Chu Hsi, 1130—1200: 麟之足不踐生草、不履生蟲、言麟性仁厚) are of Buddhist origin.

---

1) Cf. the clay tomb-figure reproduced in HENTZE, Les Figurines de la Céramique funéraire, Dresden, plate 83.

2) Cf. the detailed account in DORÉ, Recherches sur les superstitions en Chine, Part VIII, page 358—359.

3) Cf. LI-CHI, IV, 16; SHU-CHING, ch. Ku-ming, 19.

4) Cf. B. LAUFER, Chinese Clay Figures, I (Chicago 1914) pag. 114, and the literature referred to there; DORÉ, op. cit., Part II, No. 4, p. 446; Ku-chin-t'u-shu-chi-ch'eng, XV, 56, 2.

As to the flying horse Balāha[1]) (婆羅訶, explained as "Cloud-horse", yün-ma 雲馬, or "Long-haired" ch'ang-mao 長毛; the second translation refers to the reading Bālāha, Vālāha), in my opinion this is the idea that underlies the well-known Chinese ch'ih-ma 紙馬, "paper horses", *vulgo* chia-ma 甲馬, sheets of paper with some gods pictured on them, which are burnt at offerings: the divine horse carries the offerings and prayers to the gods. Chinese sources[2]) explain this usage differently; the officially adopted point of view[3]) seems to be, that the ch'ih-ma are a remnant of ancient horse-offerings at burials. First the real horses were replaced by wooden ones, and finally by horses made of paper. If this is true, then the conception of the Aerial horse (cf. the Tib. rluṅ rta, described above) will have contributed to the fact that their use was ever more extended.

In China no new traits were added to the figure of Hayagrīva. Generally he remains in the secondary place, and if he advances to the foreground it is mainly because of the fact that he is an aspect of the popular Bs. Avalokiteçvara. Traces of Chinese horse-cult connected with seri-culture have been incorporated in Buddhism, but they are connected with the famous Açvaghoṣa, the "Horse-voiced". This Bs. is usually represented as riding a horse, and he is accompanied by a woman, whose head is covered by the head of a horse, and who is called Ts'an-ming 蠶命[4]). This figure might be identical with Ma-t'ou-niang 馬頭娘, the Lady with the Horse's head, in Chinese popular religion the special goddess of sericulture[5]). This subject would necessitate a separate investigation. I could not, however, discover any connection between this conception and the figure of Hayagrīva.

Nor does there exist any connection between Hayagrīva and the Horse-headed figure that, together with a Cow-headed one, accompanies Yen-lo-wang 閻羅王, the King who presides over the fifth hell. Yen-lo-wang is the Indian Yamarāja, the King of the Dead. In Chinese popular religion he is represented with on his right side a horse-headed figure, that carries a spear with a long blade. The cow-headed figure is standing on his left side[6]). These two figures are very popular with the Chinese as demon-destroyers;

1) Cf. Buk., page 1453.

2) Cf. Doré, op. cit., Part II, No. 3, p. 297, Part XII, p. 1091.

3) Cf. Tz'ŭ-yüan, s. v.

4) Cf. Ts. P. S., part III, plate 53, 148; part IV, plate 3 and 55.

5) Cf. Doré, op. cit., part XI, p. 926 sq.

6) Cf. Doré, part VI, fig. 47; the horse-headed figure is also seen at the right of Sung-ti-wang, the King of the third hell; Mythologie Asiatique, Paris 1928, page 340.

they are called respectively Ma-mien 馬面 and Niu-t'ou 牛頭. These same two figures are the usual attendants of Ch'eng-huang 城隍, the God of Walls and Moats, who is one of the celestical Judges [1]). His cult seems to have become popular rather late, viz. during the Sung dynasty. I think these two attendants were given to him in anology with Yen-lo-wang, because Ch'eng-huang excercises a similar function. Here Ma-mien also has a human body and the head of a horse; he is holding the trident.

These two warlike attendants have been chosen out of the Twelve Holy Generals, Shih-erh sheng-chiang 十二聖將. This group is the Buddhist adaptation of the twelve ancient Chinese cyclic animals, Rat, Cow Tiger, Rabbit etc. [2]). They are represented as warriors, having human bodies but animal heads. Each carries his own special weapon: Ma-t'ou 馬頭 (this is his original appellation) holds a lance and Niu-t'ou a mace [3]). In China and Corea these twelve figures were used as guardians of tombs. A very fine statue of the horse-headed figure, carved in stone, is to be found near the King's tomb at Kyong-tju, in Corea [4]). It dates from about the eighth century, and is a splendid specimen of craftmanship. The figure is represented *en face,* and is clad in Chinese warriors attire. The right hand holds a flaming sword, whilst with the left hand he tests the sharpness of the edge. The figure has a simple horse's head, without any decoration whatever.

In the older passages of the Canon where Hayagrīva is mentioned, we find his Sanskrit name transcribed with Chinese characters. Later on, however, the Chinese translation Ma-t'ou 馬頭 becomes more usual. Then he is called Hayagrīva Mahāvidyārāja, Ma-t'ou ta-ming-wang 馬頭大明王, or Hayagrīva Avalokiteçvara, Ma-t'ou kuan-shih-yin 馬頭觀世音.

Among the material here available to me I could not find any Chinese picture of Hayagrīva. In the Japanese sources I found one picture, which represents Hayagrīva, with the special appellation "Chinese form", 唐圖; it is said that this form has been taught by Çubhākarasiṁha. Therefore I chose this picture for facing the first page of this

---

1) Cf. DORÉ, part XI, fig. 250, and the text pertaining to it.

2) Cf. Ts. P. S., part IV, plate 8—13.

3) G. MASPÉRO (in his contribution to "Mythologie Asiatique", Paris 1928, p. 349) gives for these two satellites the Sanskrit equivalents *Açvamukha* and *Goçīrṣa*, without adding an explanation as to their origin. These names are indeed exact translations of Ma-mien and Niu-t'ou; I do not know, however, on what source he relies for these equivalents. One will look for them in vain in Chinese Buddh. dictionaries.

4) Cf. ECKARDT, A History of Korean Art, London 1929, figure 153, and Ch. 9, Stone Figures by Royal Tombs.

book. In chapter IV I have reproduced some drawings taken from Japanese sources, some of which may be replica from Chinese originals. As I am not quite sure about this point, I have prefered not to use them to illustrate this Chinese chapter. I have not the slightest doubt that, apart from the pictures in Tibetan style of the Lamaist temples, in China there must exist many pictures and statues of Hayagrīva in Buddhist monasteries etc. As far as I know, however, none has been published.

In the following section of this chapter I have collected and translated the passages of the Canon where Hayagrīva is dealt with, commencing with the shorter ones and finally giving the longer text, that is exclusively devoted to his worship. Sometimes it was necessary to add some observations as to the authenticity of these texts.

I permit myself to precede the translations by some remarks about the translating of Mantrayānic texts in general.

3. Hayagrīva in the Chinese Canon

A. The Reading of the Magic Formulae (Dhāraṇī and mantra)

The reading of the magic formulae in Chinese Buddhist texts is a perilous task in more than one respect. In order to make the dhāraṇī's preserve intact their full magical force, one did not venture to translate them, but limited one's effort to the rendering of the original Indian sounds as accurately as possible. Sometimes the formulae were left standing in the Siddhaṁ-alphabet (hsi-t'an 悉曇), the favourite syllabic writing used by Chinese and Japanese Buddhists for reproducing Sanskrit words and sentences. These Siddhaṁ-characters resemble the Tibetan Lañtsha-alphabet, adapted to the Chinese brush [1]). According to Chinese usage it is written in vertical rows, from right to left (cf. the mantra reproduced in Ch. IV, 3). In reading this Siddhaṁ-texts one does not encounter much difficulty.

Mostly, however, another method was followed, viz. that of transcribing the Indian sounds, for better or for worse, by means of Chinese characters. Owing to the fundamental difference of the two languages this method was naturally accompanied by almost

---

1) For the origin of Lañtsha cf. A. H. FRANCKE, The Tibetan Alphabet (Epigraphia Indica, Vol. XI, 1911—12, p. 266). The best exposition of the Siddhaṁ-characters with all the ligatures occuring, may be found in the Japanese grammar of Sanskrit by Wogihara Unrai (荻原雲來、實習梵文學, Tōkyō 1929). Cf. further Ts. 2132 Hsi-t'an-tzŭ-chi 悉曇字記, and the following items; also the article Shittan in Mik. p. 990. For the Lañtsha-caracters cf. A. CSOMA DE KÖRÖS, Grammar of the Tibetan Language, Calcutta 1834, lithographed pages.

insuperable difficulties, for the solution of which many, often quite ingenious tricks were invented. One of these was to add various technical directions to the texts, indicating the pronunciation and intonation. Thus, for instance, the Indian sound *tra* was quite unknown in ancient Chinese. It was transcribed as 多羅 *ta-*la, with the additional remark erh-ho 二合, meaning: "combine these two!", thus making *tra* (in Chinese ears). To indicate a long vowel, such as in *tā*, one wrote 多 (引), meaning: ta (extend!), hence: *tā*. In the texts translated below many further examples may be found. As the translators who introduced these transcriptions lived in different times and in different parts of China, and as the Chinese language has always been differentiated in several widely divergent dialects, it has never been feasible to arrive at the adoption of a definite system of transcription, say in the shape of a few hundred characters which, either separately or in fixed combinations, would render definite Indian sounds. As it was, every translator used his own system, which soon led to a great confusion. Thus even the best known words are found transcribed in the most diverging ways, e.g. the word Buddha is found rendered in various texts severally as 佛陀、勃馱、沒馱、浮圖、母馱、浮屠. No single system of transcription thus being able to answer permanently to the exigences of a correct rendering, the reciting of the incantations must have been a venturesome undertaking even for the ancient Chinese Buddhists [1]).

For the modern investigator the problem becomes still more intricate. For him the modern pronunciation of the Chinese characters, which has little in common with the pronunciation which they used to connote in ancient times, must be his principal indication. Owing to the fact that the Chinese script is almost exclusively ideographic, the ancient pronunciation is only known more or less hypothetically in respect of certain localities and periods. Moreover, the transcribers or copyists often made mistakes or used variants which may have had fatal effects. If to all this is added the fact, that the original formulae were not always written in correct Sanskrit, and often were composed in later Indian dialects, or in a jumble of both, it may be understood that the reconstruction of Sanskrit texts which are thus transcribed into Chinese is a matter of great patience, and of a considerable amount of conjecture as well.

Happily there are points of support to be found in the formulae that reached us in the Siddhaṁ-script; in the translations that often accompany the formulae; and in the texts which have survived in the original Indian version, or in Tibetan transcriptions.

---

1) Chinese Buddhists therefore compiled many Sanskrit (transcribed) -Chinese Vocabularies, specimens of which may be found in Ts., part LIV.

Some western scholars, moreover, have collected many important data. As a standard-work may still be regarded Stanislas Julien, Méthode pour déchiffrer et transcrire les noms sanscrits, qui se rencontrent dans les livres chinois, Paris 1861. The edition of the Gaṇḍīstotragāthā, by Baron A. von Staël-Holstein (Biblioth. Buddhica XV, St. Petersburg 1913) is also of much use; here we find the Sanskrit, the Tibetan, and Chinese transcriptions printed side by side. O. Rosenberg in his Introduction to the Study of Buddhism (Tōkyō 1916) registers for each Chinese character the Indian sound-equivalents to which it may respond. Furthermore the Sankrit Indices of Mik. and Buk. may elucidate many doubtful cases. The first critical treatment, however, is contained in the index to the excellent paper of Sylvain Lévi, Le catalogue des Yakṣa dans le Mahāmāyūri, Journal Asiatique, 1915. Here we find the Chinese characters which are used for the phonetical rendering of the different names occurring in the text, arranged according to their modern pronunciation with the addition of the Indian sounds to which they correspond, mention being made at the same time of the author who used them for such transcription. When some authentic texts of the Canon have been treated in this manner, it will be possible then to find in the transcribed formulae important criteria for determining the authenticity of other texts. I leave out of consideration here the enormous service which such critically investigated transcriptions would render in the tracing back of the pronunciation of ancient Chinese [1]).

In the texts translated below I have, generally speaking, translated the formulae which seemed relevant to me, adding at the foot of the page the Indian reconstruction, together with the Chinese characters. The remark erh-ho after two or more characters I have replaced by + between them, and if a word was repeated, I have added (2 ×). As a rule I have not added the romanization to the Chinese characters employed to transcribe a Sanskrit word or phrase, such being of little use in the given circumstances.

The magic formulae are especially important because they have faithfully preserved the original Indian elements. We often meet in a dhāraṇī names and appellations of a deity, which in China have been forgotten altogether, and which one therefore will seek in vain in the Chinese text itself, in which the said dhāraṇī occurs (cf. p. 67, sub 116).

A special form of the mantra to which I should like to direct the attention here

1) B. Karlgren in his studies on ancient Chinese has used some Buddh. transcriptions; the way to further research in this direction has been smoothed by Yamada Takao 山田孝雄 in his "Index on all the Vocabularies of the Canon" (一切經音義索引, Tōkyō 1922).

in a few words is the mystic syllable, its shortest, and perhaps oldest from [1]).

Most of the magic formulae are introduced by means of the very ancient Indian holy sound oṁ (唵; cf. Mik., p. 193). At the end one generally finds the syllables hūṁ and phaṭ. Hūṁ (吽、合牛; cf. Mik., page 128) symbolizes strength, with special relation to the destroying of evil powers. A similar meaning is attached to the syllable phaṭ (發 吒; cf. Mik., page 1819), which means to split, to break. The sound ū (嗚; cf. Mik., p. 113) also conveys the idea of destroying. A formula usually closes with svāhā (莎 訶), "Hail!".

Many syllables, moreover, are mystic germs (S. *bīja*, Chin. chung-tzŭ, 種 子), i. e. sounds in which the essence of a deity is contained. By the meditation over this sound (inspection) one may evoke in oneself the image of a deity. So the germ hrīḥ (紇 利) represents the essence of the Bs. Avalokiteçvara. The germ of Hayagrīva is haṁ (憾; cf. Mik., p. 1821), which is analysed as ha, the initial syllable of his name, with the addition of the nasal (*anusvāra*) *ṁ*, the symbol of the universe. Sometimes we find also mentioned as his germ the germ khaṁ (欠; Mik., p. 458), explained as the first syllable of khāda "devour", a part of the special mantra of Hayagrīva (cf. page 54), again with the nasal sound added. Finally the syllable vaṁ (鑁; cf. Mik., p. 1826), the germ of the god Vairocana, is repeatedly met with in Mantrayānic texts.

Some other, less usual magic sounds are explained in footnotes to the texts.

B. The Mystic Gestures of the Hands (mudrā)

Inseparably connected with the mantra's are the mudrā's (Chin.: yin 印), literally seals, the mystic play of the hands, or manual gestures. By the making of a mudrā the mantra is sealed as it were, the word is given shape by it.

The mudrā is a special case of the belief which is spread over the entire world, that the hand, or fingers as the case may be, represent a special magic agency [2]). By the adoption of certain gestures of hands and fingers the practitioner is supposed to transform

---

1) For their meaning in Hinduism see AVALON, Shakti and Shākta, London 1929, chap. 24 and 25; id., A Garland of Letters, Varṇamālā, London 1923. For their meaning in Buddhism cf. the article A in Hob.; also STEIN, Ueber zwei Ausgaben der Saptaçatī, Wiener Zeitschrift für die Kunde des Morgenlandes, 1926.

2) For the magical meaning of manual gestures in general cf. HASTINGS, Encyclopaedia of Religion and Ethics, s. v. Hand.; "Imago", VII, p. 28, 29, 153, 154, 168, 345; ECHTERMEYER, Ueber Namen und symbolische Bedeutung der Finger bei den Griechen und Römer, 1835. For the Buddh. mudrā cf. KAWAMOURA et de MILLOUÉ, Si-do-in-dzou, Gestes de l'officiant dans les cérémonies mystiques des sectes Tendai et Singon, Paris 1899; See also P. DE KAT ANGELINO, Mudrā's op Bali, Den Haag, 1922.

himself into a conductor of the mystic forces which have been actuated by the pronouncing of the mantra.

Just as with the recital of mantra's, so with the formation of mudrā's extreme exactitude is of the greatest importance. Hence in the texts every mudrā is found described with meticulous care. Sometimes the fingers are referred to in these descriptions by the usual current Chinese names, viz. ta-chih 大指 thumb, shih-chih 食指 (or t'ou-chih 頭指) index, chung-chih 中指 middle finger, wu-ming-chih 無名指 ring finger, hsiao-chih 小指 little finger. This terminology, however, might also be understood by laymen, who might be liable to wrongly use this powerful magical instrument. Hence a more usual way is to name the fingers by their secret, mystic apellations. In the She-ta-i-kuei [1]) 攝大儀軌, translated by Amoghavajra, these mystic values are explained as follows: "The ten fingers are the Ten Virtues of Perfection (S. *pāramitā*), or also they are called the ten Essential Worlds (S. *dharmadhātu*), or also the tenfold Truth (S. *tathatā*). When folded together they form one entity, but when spread out they have different names. The left little finger is called Charity (t'an, S. *dāna*), the ring finger is called Morality (chieh, S. *çīla*), the left middle finger is called Resignation (jen, S. *kṣānti*), the left fore finger is called Energy (chin, S. *vīrya*), the left thumb is called Meditation (chan, S. *dhyāna*). The right little finger is called Understanding (hui, S. *prajñā*), the ring finger is called the Means (fang, S. *upāya*), the right middle finger is called the Vows (yüän, S. *praṇidhāna*), the right fore finger is called Power (li, S. *bala*), the right thumb is called Knowledge (chih, S. *jñāna*)" [2]). Besides this system others are mentioned, the description of which I need not enter into here, as in the texts translated below only the system described above is used, varied with the ordinary everyday names [3]). Further the left hand is sometimes indicated by the mystic name ting 定, the right hand by the appellation hui 慧.

I shall, however, have to dwell slightly on the special names of different gestures of the hand, which repeatedly occur in the texts.

---

1) Ts. 1067, where the original, very long title may be found.

2) Ts. XX, page 129: 十指卽十度。或名十法界。或曰十真如。縮則攝收一。開則有數名。左小指爲檀。無名指爲戒。左中指爲忍。左頭指爲進。左大指爲禪。右小指爲慧。無名指爲方。右中指爲願。右頭指爲力。右大指爲智。

3) In the translation of the Chinese texts I have added the Chinese pronunciation in brackets to the names of the fingers, where these were denoted by their mystic names.

In the first place six kinds of fists[1]), liu chung ch'uan 六種拳 are distinguished, viz.:

1. Lotus-fist, lien-hua-ch'uan 蓮花拳, S. *padma-muṣṭi*. The fist is clenched with the thumb outside, pressed against the fore finger.

2. Vajra-fist, chin-kang-ch'uan 金剛拳, S. *vajra-muṣṭi*. The fist is clenched with the thumb folded inside the other fingers.

3. Turned-outwards, wai-fu 外縛, S. *bahir-bandhana*. The fingers of both hands are entwined together in such a way that the tops of the fingers of each hand rest on the back of the other hand.

4. Turned-inwards, nei-fu 內縛, S. *antara-bandhana*. The fingers of both hands are entwined in such a way that the fingertops of both hands are invisible.

5. Anger-fist, fen-nu-ch'uan 忿怒拳, S. *krodha-muṣṭi*. The little finger and the index finger are bent hook-wise, the ring finger and middle finger are folded down over the thumb turned inward over the palm of the hand.

6. Tathāgata-fist, ju-lai-ch'uan 如來拳, S. *tathāgata-muṣṭi*. The left hand is clenched to a fist with the thumb pointing upwards, which is then enclosed by the right hand.

The belief in the magical force of the *krodha-muṣṭi* is spread over the entire world. Cf. HASTINGS, op. cit., *sub voce* Hand:"....the most common is the mano cornuta, in which the index and little fingers are extended to imitate horns, the others being bent over and clasped by the thumb. This gesture is both ancient and wide-spread in its use. It is represented in early Christian art as a gesture of the hand symbolizing the Deity". Further it is used especially against the evil eye. Also in Buddhism this gesture will scare away demons and evil influences.

Both hands folded together in some way or other are called ho-chang 合掌, S. *añjali*. In Hinduism the *añjali* is nothing else than placing the hollowed hands together in respectful greeting. In Buddhism, however, this term seems to be very loosely used, meaning any posture of both hands together generally. Once I found ho-chang transcribed as *yamaka*, "pair", which seems to be a better appellation.

Twelve special ho-chang are distinguished, each of which has a separate name (cf. Him., p. 452, and Mik., p. 879). Some of this group occur in our texts, and are described there.

---

1) Cf. Mik., page 2316.

C. Shorter References

1. Mahāvairocana-sūtra 大毘盧遮那成佛神變加持經 (Ts. 848), translated by Çubhākarasiṁha and I Hsing (cf. *supra*, page 25, 26).

Ch. I, page 6 and 7, Avalokiteçvara is described as forming part of a maṇḍala. To his right is Tārā, to his left Bhṛkuṭī, and in front of him Hayagrīva.

"In front of the Holy One one should paint the Very Strong Vidyārāja (大力持明王) Hayagrīva (何耶揭利婆). His colour should be like that of the sun, rising at dawn. White lotus-flowers adorn his body. He is surrounded by garlands of bright fire. He should have a fierce appearance, showing his bare fangs. He has sharp nails, and the mane of a lion" [1]).

ibidem, chapter II, page 14:

"The mantra of Hayagrīva runs: Hail to all the Buddha's! Hūṁ! Devour! Break! Destroy! Svāhā. (S.: *namo samanta buddhānām hūṁ khāda bhañja sphaṭya svāhā*, Chin.: 南麼三曼多勃馱喃𤙖佉陀畔闍薩＋破吒＋也莎訶).

2. Ta-jih-ching-shu 大日經疏 (Ts. 1796), an extensive commentary on the Mahāvairocana-sūtra, written by I Hsing. On page 632 the passage quoted above is explained in the following way:

"Beneath the Bs. Lok. one should then place Hayagrīva. This name means: Horse's head. The colour of his body is between yellow and red, just like the colour of the sun at dawn. He is adorned with white lotus-flowers and other ornaments. He wears a flaming effulgence as garland. His nails are long and sharp, his face shows a pair of bare fangs. His hair is like the mane of a lion. He has an extremely fierce appearance. This is the fierce Vidyārāja of the Lotus-section. He is just like the Horse-jewel (ma-pao 馬寶, S. *açvaratna*) of a Cakravartin, that wanders about the four continents, nowhere and never giving itself one moment rest, having the great force of all the Bs. Just like this is his nature, and therefore he possesses this terrible might. Amidst the obstacles of birth and death he is without the slightest care for his own welfare, and therefore many submit to him. This is because of his pure heart full of compassion. And therefore his body is adorned with white lotus-flowers".

---

1) The Tibetan text of this passage runs: deḥi ḥog tu sṅags pa yis. rigs sṅags rgyal po stobs po che. kha dog ñi ma ḥchar ka bṣin. padma dkar po rnam par rgyan. ḥbar baḥi phreṅ can mi bzad ciṅ. spu dag seṅ ge ltar hdug pa. sbyan ras gzigs dbaṅ blo ldan gyi. rta mgrin can ṣes grags pa bri. (cf. the critical edition of the Tib. text of the Ta-jih-ching, by Hattori, 1931, p. 68).

3. Wu-liang-shou-ju-lai-kuan-hsing-kung-yang-i-kuei 無量壽如來觀行供養儀軌 (Ts. 930), translated by Amoghavajra.

Page 69: "Then one should make the mudrā of the Bs. Hayagrīva Lok. One should first make the añjali for marking off the place (i. e. the hands are laid with the palms against each other, while the middle fingers and little fingers are erected straight), that discards all evil influences. Then one should bend both forefingers and both ring fingers into the palm of the hand, their nails touching each other. Both thumbs should be bent slightly, without, however, touching the forefingers. Then the mudrā is formed [1]). One should chant the mtr. of the Vidyārāja Hayagrīva, that runs: Oṁ! He who is born from nectar! Hūṁ phaṭ svāhā! (S.: *oṁ amṛtodbhava hūṁ phaṭ svāhā*, Chin.: 唵阿密+栗妬納+婆嚩吽發吒娑+嚩賀).

When one has chanted this mtr. three times, swinging round the hands folded in the above-described mdr. three times to the left, then all demons and all evil influences will be dispersed. Having swung round the mdr. three times to the right, the Immovable Sphere (堅固界) will be effected [2]).

4. P'u-t'i-ch'ang-so-shuo-i-tzŭ-ting-lun-wang-ching 菩提場所說一字頂輪王經 (Ts. 950), translated by Amoghavajra.

Page 199: "On the right side of the Bs. Lok. one should paint the Mahāvidyārāja Hayagrīva (賀耶仡哩嚩大明王). His colour should be made like fire, and he should have a fierce appearance. His nose should be like that of a monkey. He should be adorned with snakes, and wear all ornaments like arm-rings and rings round the wrists, while his head is adorned with a wreath of lotus-flowers.

5. She-wu-ai-ching 攝無礙經 (Ts. 1067), translated by Amoghavajra.

Page 131: "Then Hayagrīva Lok.: on top of his head he bears the head of the Açvaratna. He has three faces, each face having three eyes. The middle face bears on its crest the image of a Buddha of Transformation (hua-fu 化佛). His body has a bright flesh-colour. His appearance is extremely fierce, his bare fangs biting the lips. He has four arms and two feet. The left and right hand each show a mudrā. The left hand shows the Brilliant Fist (kuang-chieh-ch'uan 光結拳). The left little finger is bent over the ring and middle finger, while fore finger and thumb are erected so as to form the shape of a beak. With the right hand one should make the same gesture. Both fore

1) This mdr. is said to represent the form of a horse's mouth, ma-k'ou-hsing 馬口形.

2) chien-ku-chieh, a sacred sphere, not to be shaken by any demon or evil spirit.

fingers should touch each other. This mdr. is made a little below the breast. The next left hand also shows a mdr., whilst the next right hand shows the axe. The Bs. is splendidly adorned with garlands. He is clad in heavenly garments, that shine with a wonderful crystal colour. He is sitting cross-legged on a lotus flower, the right leg pressing the left."

6. Pa-tzŭ-wen-shu-kuei 八字文殊軌 (Ts. 1184), translated by Bodhiṛṣi, circa 800 A.D.

On page 785 the altar of Mañjuçrī-of-the-eight-syllables (S. *aṣṭabīja*) is described. On each corner a Vidyārāja is standing: Trailokavijaya (降三世), Mahābalaguṇa (大威德), Ajita (無能勝), and Hayagrīva.

"At the north-eastern corner one should paint the Vidyārāja Hayagrīva. He should have three faces, and eight arms. Each hand holds an instrument. The left upper hand is holding a lotus-flower, the next holds the amṛta-jar, and with the other he is holding the staff against his breast. The remaining left hand is entwined with the corresponding right hand in a mudrā. The upper right hand carries the axe, the next one holds the rosary (shu-chu 數珠, S. *jāpamālā*), and the other the noose.

7. Pu-k'ung-chuan-so-shen-pien-chen-yen-ching 不空羂索神變眞言經 (Ts. 1092), translated by Bodhiruci, circa 650 A.D.

Page 271: "Then the Bs. Hayagrīva Lok. His left hand holds the axe, his right hand the stalk of a lotus-flower. He is sitting cross-legged."

D. The longer text of the T'o-lo-ni-chi-ching

The fundamental text which in the Chinese Canon is devoted to Hayagrīva is to be found in the "Collection of Dhāraṇī" (Ts. 901, 陀羅尼集經, S. *Dhāraṇī-saṁgraha* [1]). The greater part of the sixth chapter of this work particularly treats of the figure of Hayagrīva.

This Dhāraṇī-saṁgraha seems to me to be an authentic text, translated directly from the Sanskrit. This may be concluded especially on account of the style, an awkward and therefore often not easily comprehensible Chinese. The translator was the Indian priest Atikūṭa [2]) (阿地瞿多, translated as wu-chi-kao 無極高; cf. Mik., p. 14), regarding whom various sources furnish elaborate data.

1) This is only a tentative reconstruction of the original Sanskrit title, if there was any. Hob. F. A., p. 51 proposes *Dhāraṇī-samuccaya*.

2) Hob. F. A., p. 128 uses Atigupta; but I think Atikūṭa, given by Mik., accords better with the Chinese translation.

The earliest mention of the Dhāraṇī-saṁgraha occurs in the catalogue Ta-chou-k'an-ting-chung-ching-mu-lu 大周刊定衆經目錄 (Ts. 2153), compiled by Ming Ch'uan 明佺, who worked in Lo-yang about 700. In chapter I, page 379 we find mentioned that the work contains 12 chapters, and was translated in 651 by Atikūṭa in the Hui-jih monastery 慧日寺, at Ch'ang-an.

Furthermore we find it mentioned in the great catalogue K'ai-yüan-shih-chiao-mu-lu 開元釋教目錄 (Ts. 2154), compiled by Chih Sheng 智昇 (698—740). In chapter 8, page 562, biographical details concerning Atikūṭa are given.

The catalogue Cheng-yüan-hsin-ting-shih-chiao-mu-lu 貞元新定釋教目錄 (2157), compiled by Yüan Chao 圓照 (end of 8th century) repeats word for word the article from the K'ai-yüan catalogue.

A short biography of Atikūṭa is furthermore contained in chapter 2 of "Biographies of famous priests, compiled during the Sung-dynasty" (Sung-kao-seng-ch'uan 宋高僧傳, Ts. 2061).

To the Dhāraṇī-saṁgraha an Introduction has been added, which is said to have been written by a priest Hsüan K'ai 玄楷 (or 揩), who furnishes therein a short description of the life of Atikūṭa, and further narrates how he himself had written down Atikūṭa's translation from the Sanskrit.

When we now compare, however, these various notes on the Dhāraṇī-saṁgraha and its author, we must conclude that the data given in the K'ai-yüan Catalogue have formed the material both for the biography in the Sung-kao-seng-ch'uan and for the Introduction, which is alleged to have been written by Hsüan K'ai. The K'ai-yüan text mentions Atikūṭa as the author, and Hsüan K'ai as the scribe. Unhappily I have not been able to find further particulars relating to this Hsüan K'ai. In the Introduction accredited to him he is introduced in the first person. If, however, the K'ai-yüan text and the Introduction are laid side by side, it is plain that this Introduction is nothing more than a literary recast and elaboration of the K'ai-yüan text (in which Hsüan K'ai is only mentioned in the third person). This Introduction must be a later production, probably the work of some Chinese priest, which was to give the impression of having been written by Hsüan K'ai, the scribe himself, the intention being to enhance the authority of the Dhāraṇī-saṁgraha still further.

In the following translations I first give the K'ai-yüan text, and then the Introduction said to be of Hsüan K'ai.

Collection of Dhāraṇī's, in twelve chapters.

The priest [1]) Atikūṭa, in Chinese: the Extremely High One, was a man from Central India. In his study he learned thoroughly all kinds of writing, in his conduct he was pure like a flawless pearl. He could grasp the essence of the Five Kinds of Knowledge [2]), and miraculously penetrate the Threefold Canon. Next to these qualities he possessed the inclination natural to all great men, to benefit all creatures; so he did not grudge his wisdom to other countries. His intention was to propagate the Buddhist Doctrine [3]), forgetting all fear of hardship and danger. Parted from the West he traversed the Snowy Mountains, and in the East he crossed the sandy desert. Having sustained all hardships he reached China (?) [4]). In the year 652 [5]), the first month, he arrived at Ch'ang-an, with a great many books in Sanskrit. On Imperial command he settled down in the Tz'ŭ-en monastery. The priest Ta-sheng-tsung and others, sixteen in all, and also Prince Ying [6]) and Prince Ao [7]) and others, together twelve people, they all asked Atikūṭa to establish in the Buddha-hall of the Hui-jih monastery an "Altar of the Collected Dhāraṇī's." All the accessories of the said altar were arranged there by them. On the day the method was practised several mystic phenomena manifested themselves. The priests and citizens in the capital all exclaimed that they had seldom seen the like. The priest Hsüan K'ai and others besought him eagerly to translate the manual for this

陀羅尼集經十二卷。沙門阿地瞿多、唐言無極高、中印度人。學窮滿字、行潔圓珠。精練五明、妙通三藏。加以大士利生、無恪鄉國。志弘像教、罔懼難險。遂西踰雪嶺、東越沙河。載歷艱難來儀帝闕。以天皇永徽三年壬子正月、廣將梵本、來屆長安。勅令慈恩寺安置。沙門大乘琮等一十六人、英公鄂公等一十二人、請高於慧日寺浮圖院、建陀羅尼普集會壇。緣壇所須並皆供辦。法成之日屢降靈異。京中道俗咸歎希逢。沙門玄楷等、遂固請翻其法

---

1) sha-men, S. *çramaṇa.*

2) wu-ming, S. *pañca-vidyā.*

3) Hsiang-chiao, cf. Pelliot in Journal Asiatique, 1916, II, p. 194

4) i-ti-ch'üeh; dictionaries nor the ordinary reference-works (like P'ei-wen-yün-fu) give this term.

5) Hob. F. A., p. 128, has 625, an evident misprint.

6) Li Shih-chi 李世勣, tzu: Mou-kung 懋功, cf. T'ang-shu 唐書, 93, p. 5 recto.

7) Wei-ch'ih Ching-te 尉遲敬德, cf. T'ang-shu, 89, p. 3 recto.

method. Then, from 653 till 654, in the Hui-jih monastery he chose the most important parts out of the Chin-kang-ta-tao-ch'ang-ching[1]), and translated them. These extracts he collected in twelve chapters. The priest Hsüan K'ai and others acted thereby as pi-shou[2]).

In that time the priest Master Anurudhamokṣa, the Master Kaçyapa and others, of the Mahābodhi monastery in Central India, had translated the "Method for worshipping Lakṣmī-devī"[3]) in the Ching-hsing monastery. This was inserted in the tenth chapter; therefore it has not been preserved elsewhere.

Introduction to the translation of the Collection of Dhāraṇī's, promulgated by Buddha.

The doctrine[4]) of the magic spells, the mystic gestures and the altar (belonging to them) is indeed the heart and marrow of all the sūtra's. It is the leading tenet of all the various magical practises. Its outlines are extremely profound and secret, beyond the reach of superficial knowledge. Its meaning is mysterious and abstruse, thoughts cannot fathom it. It is a secret among secrets, indescribable!

There was a priest of high virtue, called Atikūṭa, a man from Central India. The cleverness and wisdom of this Master of the Law were quite out of the common, whilst in virtue he surpassed all men. Since his twentieth year he cherished the (Buddhist)

本。後以四年癸丑至五年甲寅於慧日寺、從金剛大道場經中撮要鈔譯。集成十二卷。沙門玄楷等筆受。于時有中印度大菩提寺僧阿難律木叉師、迦葉師等、於經行寺譯功德天法。編在集經第十卷內、故不別存也。

佛說陀羅尼集經翻譯序。若夫陀羅尼印壇法門者、斯迺衆經之心髓、引萬行之導首。宗深祕密、非淺識之所知。義趣冲玄、匪思慮之能測。密中更密、無得稱焉。

有高德沙門、厥號阿地瞿多。是中天竺人也。法師聰慧超羣、德邁過人。弱冠慕

1) I could nowhere find more details concerning this work, the original title of which might be something like *Vajra-mahā-bodhi-maṇḍa-sūtra*.

2) Pi-shou was the title of the copyist, who wrote down the text from the mouth of the translator (the chih-pen 執本), at the same time perfecting the style. For the methods followed in China in translating Indian texts, cf. the article by W. Fuchs, Zur technischen Organisation der Uebersetzungen buddhistischer Schriften ins Chinesische, in „Asia Maior", Vol. VI, 1930, p. 84.

3) Cf. Dhāraṇī-saṁgraha, p. 874, and Mik. p. 346.

4) fa-men, *dharmaparyāya*.

Doctrine, and rambled through the five parts of India, looking for kindred spirits. Very humbly he wandered on, searching for the principles of the Law. Therefore he could grasp the essence of the Five Kinds of Knowledge, and miraculously penetrate all sections of the Canon. Then he wished to transport the Water of the Law of the Western regions, and moisten therewith those who were thirstingly looking forward to it in the East, in China. He risked his life in dangers and hardships, intent on preserving the pith of the Grand Doctrine. He traversed steep mountains without being tired, he crossed the desert without being fatigued. Carrying on his head the venerable Scriptures, he came to this Chinese land. In the year 651 [1]), in the first month, he arrived at Ch'ang-an, and on Imperial command he settled down in the Tz'ŭ-men [2]) monastery. When the Master of the Law had not yet said anything, he was not unlike a jewel, cherished in the bosom. When he pronounced his elegant discussions, however, the treasures of his knowledge were known. Therefore he could decide all doubts (settle all doubtful questions) and explain all right principles.

There had been more than one who transmitted the Sūtra's, the Discipline, the Principles of the Doctrine, and the Magical Acts [3]), but this School (i. e. the Mantrayāna) had not yet prospered in China. Therefore, when eagerly besought three times, he at last taught the rules for making (magical) altars. During the first ten days of the third month he went to the Hui-jih cloister; in the Buddha-hall the Master of the Law himself made the "Altar of the Collected Dhāraṇī's". There Ta-sheng-tsung and others, sixteen in all, and also Prince Ying and Prince Ao and others, twelve people in all, assisted him while he was officiating, and all together pronounced vows for the everlasting prosperity of the

道、歷五竺而尋友。低心躍步、而諮法要。故能精練五明、妙通諸部。意欲運西域之法水、潤東夏之渴仰。判身許于險難、務存弘道之心。跋山巖而不疲、涉沙流而無倦。頂戴尊經、向斯漢地。永徽二年正月、屆于長安、奉勅住慈門寺。但法師含珠未吐、人莫別于懷珍。雅辯旣宣方知有寶。故能決衆疑、言皆當理。然則經律論業傳者非一、唯此法門未興斯土。所以丁寧三請方許壇法。三月上旬赴慧日寺、浮圖院內、法師自作普集會壇、大乘琮等一十六人、爰及英公鄂公等一十二人、助成壇供。同願皇基永

1) Ts. 2154 has 652.

2) Ts. 2154 has Tz'ŭ-en.

3) S.: *Sūtra*, *vinaya*, *abhidharma* and *karma-vidyā* (?)

Imperial House; that it might reach all countries, and benefit alike all classes, in order to bring them great bliss. The holy auguries effected by this ceremony were so numerous, that I am afraid I can not record them all.

When I was fortunate enough to become acquainted with this Doctrine, I could not but dance from sheer joy. I went personally to the place where the books were translated, with the intention to ask him to translate the whole work. But at that time he was very busy, and I could not formulate my demands. Then, fearing that the abstruseness of the matter would bring him to refuse, and thus great benefit would be lost, in the Hui-jih monastery I asked the Master of the Law to promulgate a translation of the Sanskrit text, and write down a translation of the most important parts, together twelve chapters, in order to make prosperous the great foundation of the empire, and to preserve secret treasure that elevates the people below. He set to work on the 14th day of the third month, 653, and on the fifteenth day of the fourth month, 654, his task was finished. Afterwards the Master of the Law was summoned repeatedly to the Palace. During our casual meetings he had no leisure to look over the text again with me.

This book is an extract from the Chin-kang-ta-tao-ch'ang-ching, and it forms but a small section of the Great Mantra-piṭaka. I have tried now to correct these general outlines; I offer them hoping that they may widely circulate and become known all over the Empire.

固、常臨萬國、庶類同沾、皆成大益。其中靈瑞、恐繁不述。余慶逢此法、不勝欣躍。躬詣翻經所悕翻廣本。屢値事鬧、不及陳請。恐幻質遷謝、失于大利、便請法師于慧日寺、宣譯梵本且翻要抄、一十二卷。竪輿國之洪基、存隆民之祕寶歟。從四年三月十四日起首、至永徽五年歲次甲寅四月十五日畢。以後頻頻勅追法師入內。邂逅之間、無暇復校。

此經出金剛大道場經、大明咒藏分之少分也。今此略抄擬勘詳定、奏請流通天下普聞焉。

The Dhāraṇī-saṁgraha is composed in the well-known saṁgīti-form. It commences with the narration of how Buddha, in the midst of a throng of gods, saints and disciples, teaches in Çrāvastī 舍衛國 different rites for the attainment of siddhi's. In succession a countless number of gods and goddesses are described, and the ritual for their worship is given, with mention of their special mantra's and mudrā's and elaborate data regarding their appearance. These latter descriptive passages are particularly important from an iconographic point of view.

Chapter 5 then treats of different forms of Avalokiteçvara. Then Bhṛkuṭī is described, and after that, chapter 6 in keeping with the regular order deals with Hayagrīva, as an aspect of Avalokiteçvara. This text forms by itself a self-contained entity. From the uniformity of style and composition and on the strength of some references to previous chapters, it may be plainly seen that this text originally belongs to the Dhāraṇīsaṁgraha.

Section regarding the Mudrā's and Mantra's to be used for worshipping the Bodhisattva Hayagrīva Avalokiteçvara, **何耶揭唎婆觀世音菩薩法印咒品.**

1. Mudrā and mantra for protecting one's body[1] and for marking off the place[2], while worshipping Hayagrīva, **馬頭護身結界法印咒.**

The middle-, ring- and little finger of each hand should be forked in each other, turned outwards, each fingertop tapping the back of the other hand. This is the añjali[3]. Both forefingers should be erected straight, being about $^1/_2$ inch apart from each other. The two thumbs are touching each other, the knuckle bent. They should not touch the forefingers. Moving the forefingers to and fro, one should chant the mtr.:

Oṁ! The glowing rays of the blown vajra! Hail![4]

These are the mdr. and mtr. If one wishes to receive the discipline of this Bs., one should begin with protecting one's body by making this mdr., and the chanting of this mtr. One should chant the mtr. seven times over pieces of wood, or also seven times over water. Then one makes the mdr. over the water. One may also chant the mtr. over white mustard-seed. If one says the mtr. over ashes or the like, in any case one should repeat the mtr. seven times, and make the mdr. over them. At the four corners of the

---

1) hu-shen **護身**, S. *ātmarakṣa*, a ceremony which makes the body of the practitioner immune from all evil influences. Cf. Mik., p. 609.

2) chieh-chieh **結界**, tr. **畔陀也死曼** S. *bandhaya-sīman* (corresponding to the Hinduist *sīma-bandhana*) is the name of a ceremony which marks off a special place to be used for an offering, excluding all evil influences from it. Cf. Mik., p. 451.

3) ho-chang **合掌.**

4) *oṁ pravikasita vajra jvala-raci svāhā*, **唵鉢+囉毘迦悉跢跋折+囉涉+筏囉囉支莎訶.**

altar one should erect the pieces of wood, thus marking off the place. If one scatters the mustard-seed, the ashes and the water in the ten directions, also in this way the marking off of the place will be effected. When afterwards one performs the other rites, one will get a manifestation (i. e. of the god).

2. Mdr. and mtr. of the Great Essential Body[1]) of Hayagrīva, 馬頭大法身印咒.

The fore-finger, middlefinger and ringfinger of each hand should be forked in each other, turned outwards, the tops tapping the back of the other hand. This is the *añjali*. The two little fingers should be stretched out together, the thumbs should touch each other, being strongly bent. Moving the thumbs to and fro, one should say the mtr.:

Oṁ! Shake, shake! Crush, crush! Devour, devour! Hayagrīva! ū hūṁ phaṭ, hail[2])!

These are the mdr. and mtr. If one is bitten by a venomous insect or by a snake, or injured by bad people, one will be cured by making the mdr. and chanting the mtr.

There is another method if one wishes to make the clouds[3]) come. One should take sumana-flowers[4]), and before the image of Hgr. chant 21 times the mtr. over them, scattering them over the feet of the image. Taking the flowers with the right hand, one may scatter them over the place where one is practising, wherever one likes. When the clouds are gone, after having repeated the mtr. seven times over the flowers, and then scattering them, they will come again. There is also a method, if one wishes to rouse love between two people. One should take fruits and repeat the mtr. 21 times over them. When one makes people eat these, their hearts will become confused, and they will love each other fervently, having no thought for anything else.

---

1) ta-fa-shen 大法身, S. *mahā-dharma-kāya*.

2) *oṁ dhūna dhūna matha matha khāda khāda hayagrīva ū hūṁ phaṭ svāhā*, Chin. 唵杜那(2×)摩他(2×)可馱(2×)訶耶揭+唎婆嗚吽柿莎訶. The standard dictionary of K'ang-hsi gives as pronunciation of 柿: p'o, that might correspond with an older *phat. As moreover *hūṁ phaṭ*, is the usual ending of the magic formulae, I have adopted the transcription phaṭ, although the variants read 泮, that seems to suggest haṁ.

3) me-ku 咩古; this transcription is indeed a riddle to me. Perhaps 古 is a misprint for 茄, the whole standing for S. *megha*, cloud, the summoning of rain-clouds being a magical feat much practised by Mantrayānic priests (cf., for instance, the biography of *Amoghavajra*, in Sung-kao-seng-ch'uan 宋高僧傳). But I admit this interpretation is very questionable.

4) 蘇摩那華, a yellow, odoriferous flower; cf. Mik., p. 1328, and P. W., s. v.

3. Mdr. and mtr. of the Essential Heart[1]) of Hayagrīva, 馬頭法心印咒.

The fore finger, middle finger, ring finger and little finger of each hand should be forked into each other, turned outwards, the tops tapping the back of the other hand. This is the *añjali*. Both thumbs should touch each other, bent at the knuckle. They should not touch the forefingers. Moving the thumbs to and fro, one should say the mtr.:

Oṁ! He who is born of nectar! ū hūṁ phaṭ svāhā[2])!

These are the mdr. and mtr. When one wishes to have a dispute, one should take the three perfumes *gorocanā*[3]), musk[4]) and camphor[5]), and rub them together, chanting the mantra eightthousand times. With this mixture one should make spots on the top of one's head, on both of one's shoulders, on heart and throat, between the eyebrows, and at the back of one's head, where the hair ceases to grow. Then one should take white mustard-seed, and repeat the mtr. thirty seven times over it. This mustard-seed one should take in the right hand. At the place where the dispute will be held, one should scatter them by the side of the door; some, however, one should keep in one's left hand. At the time of the dispute, one should take with the right hand the seeds from the left hand, and secretly throw them at the man who is disputing. If one then snaps one's fingers, one will vanquish him. The method is like this.

4. Mudrā and Mantra of the head of Hayagrīva, 馬頭頭法印咒.

One should make the mdr. of protecting the body described above, with this difference that one makes the tops of the forefingers touch each other, both being bent. One brings the two thumbs forward, and pointing them towards each other at the top, one says the mtr.: ***.

The method is like this: when anyone is suffering from head-ache, one should take a slip with his name written on it, and chant the mtr. over water. Having uttered the sounds *ū hūṁ*, one should throw this water over the head of the patient. Then, having made the mdr. over the sore place, the pain will be cured.

---

1) fa-hsin 法心, S. *dharma-cittā.*

2) *oṁ amṛtodbhava ū hūṁ phaṭ svāhā,* 唵阿蜜+唎都知+婆婆鳴合牛柿莎訶.

3) niu-huang 牛黃, yellow pigment, made from the bile of a cow.

4) che-hsiang 麝香.

5) lung-nao 龍腦, litt. dragon-brains.

5. Mudrā and Mantra of the top of the head of Hayagrīva, 馬頭頂法印咒.

One should make first the head-mudrā, erecting, however, both fore-fingers, the tops touching each other. The middle-fingers should both be stretched out, in front of the fore-fingers, touching their tops. One should say the mtr.: * * *.

These are the mdr. and mtr. When anyone is suffering from pain at the top of his head, one should make this mdr. over the sore place. Having chanted the mtr., the pain will vanish.

6. Mudrā and Mantra of the mouth of Hayagrīva, 馬頭口法印咒.

The ring finger and the little finger of each hand one should fork in each other, and bend them into the palms of the hands. Both middle fingers one should erect straight, the tops touching each other. The two thumbs should be erected also. The right fore-finger should touch the right thumb. The left fore-finger is erected, slightly bent, by the side of the middle-finger. The mtr. runs: * * *.

This mdr. and mtr. one can use for curing all kinds of diseases caused by devils; they will vanish.

7. Mudrā and Mantra of the teeth of Hayagrīva, 馬頭牙法印咒.

One should make first the teeth-mudrā of the Bs. Lok. Amoghapāça[1]). The two middle fingers, however, should be erected straight, the tops touching each other. The two thumbs should be also erected, tapping the middle fingers. One should first with the left little finger touch the back of the right ring finger, and then the back of the right little finger. One should say the mtr.:

Hail to the three Jewels! Hail to the noble Avalokiteçvara! To the Bodhisattva! To the Great Being! To the Great Compassionate One! Thus[2]): (etc., see in the footnote).

---

1) This mdr. is described in Chapter V of the *Dhāraṇī-saṁgraha*, under 12, as a variation of the mouth-mudrā of Amoghapāça, which is rather complicated: "the two little fingers should be erected straight. The right ring finger is twisted behind the left ring- and middle finger, and brought between the fore- and middle finger. The left ring finger is stuck forward between the right middle- and ring finger, and then brought between the fore- and middle finger. The two middle fingers are erected straight, the tops touching each other. The two fore fingers are bent, each hooking over the ring fingers. The two thumbs are erect, the tops touching each other, at a distance of about half an inch away from the little fingers". The teeth-mudrā is formed by bending in this mdr. the two middle fingers a little, so that each presses the top of the thumb. The two little fingers should be sticking out, the right one pressing the left, touching the back of the ring finger. Surely one needs the nimble fingers of an oriental to reproduce this mudrā.

2) *namo ratna-trayāya nama āryāvalokiteçvarāya bodhisattvāya mahāsattvāya mahākaruṇikāya tadyathā*

This mdr. and mtr. should be used for breaking the force of all kinds of spells. It one wishes to make the charms said by other people powerless, one should make a three-coloured flour-altar, measuring four cubits square. On the north- and the south-side one should paint a lotus-seat. On these lotus-seats one should paint the shape of a tooth. On the east-side one should also paint a lotus-seat, and thereon a *vajra-mudrā*. One should kindle twelve lamps, and prepare eight dishes of delightful fruit and food. Having eaten these on the next day one should put on new clothes, and make new offerings, continuing in this way till seven days have elapsed. The next day one should say the mtr. 108 times over white mustard-seed, each time one says the mtr. burning one seed in the fire. Now all spells said by other people [1]) will be without any effect.

8. Mudrā and Mantra for begging food while invoking Hayagrīva, **馬頭觀世音菩薩乞食法印咒**.

One should lift up the left hand, with the five fingers stretched out. The right hand is hanging downwards, the tops of middle finger, ring finger and thumb touching each other. The mtr. runs: * * *.

It should be chanted twenty-seven times.

9. Mudrā and Mantra for warding off a sword while invoking Hayagrīva, **馬頭觀世音菩薩解禁刀法印咒**.

One should stretch out both hands, the left hand with the palm turned outwards, the right hand inwards. With the left hand one should support the back of the right. The two thumbs should be erected. The mtr. is: * * *.

10. Mudrā and Mantra for curing diseases while invoking Hayagrīva, **馬頭療病法印咒**.

The ring- and little finger of both hands one should fork in each other, bent into the palm of the hand. The two middle fingers one should erect, the tops touching each other. One should bend the thumb right in front of them. With the two fore fingers one should touch the thumbs at the base of the nail, while the nails of the fore fingers are touching each other. The mtr. is: (same as quoted sub 6). This mdr. and mtr. should be used to

---

traṭa (2×) *tama* (2×) *cintā* (2×) *piṇḍa* (2×) *ū hūṁ phaṭ phaṭ svāhā*, 南謨囉跢+那怛+囉夜耶 (1) id. 阿梨+耶婆盧吉帝+攝+婆囉耶 (2) 菩提薩埵耶 (3) 摩訶 id. (4) id. 迦嚧尼迦耶 (5) 跢姪他 (6) 跢+囉吒 (7) 末吒 (8) 瞋陀 (9) 頻陀 (10).

1) "Other people" is explained by a naive commentary as: non-Buddhist, bad people (餘人者謂外道惡人).

cure all kinds of diseases, and for all suffering caused by evil spirits. All will be cured, and the disease will vanish.

11. The great Mantra of the Bs. Hayagrīva Avalokiteçvara, **馬頭觀世音菩薩大咒**.

1. Hail to the three Jewels! 2. Hail to the noble Lok.! 3. To the Bodhisattva! 4. To the Great Being! 5. To the great Compassionate One! 6. Hail to the destroyer of the sins of all beings! 8. Hail to him who delivers all beings from fear! 9. Hail to him who sets at rest the fears of all beings! 10. Hail to him who cures the maladies of all beings! 11. Hail to him who breaks the bonds of all beings! 12. Hail to him who effectuates for all beings the delivery from misery and distress . . . !

(The numbers 13—56 contain other epitheta of Lok., and continue then with an enumeration of Hindu-gods, Viṣṇu, Maheçvara, Nārāyaṇa, Çiva, Skandha, Kubera etc.; among magical formulae the name Hayagrīva occurs once. Then there follow some fragments of special formulae of Hayagrīva:)

57. To the Devourer of wrong knowledge! . . . 59. Do homage! Do homage! 60. Venerable Hayagrīva! 61. Devour! Devour! . . . 75. Clutch everything! . . . 105. Do! Do! 106. To Hayagrīva, phaṭ! 107. To the Vajra-hook, phaṭ! 108. Ruin, phaṭ! 109. To the Vajra-fang, phaṭ! . . . 112. Destroy all bad spells, phaṭ! . . . 116. To the Horse-faced One!

(The formula closes with the usual:)

hūṁ hūṁ phaṭ phaṭ svāhā!

---

1. namo ratnatrayāya 2. nama āryāvalokiteçvarāya 3. bodhisattvāya 4. mahāsattvāya 5. mahākaruṇikāya 6. namaḥ sarva-sattva-vyasana-ghāṭine 7. namaḥ sarva-sattva-vyasanāpahārine 8. nama sarva-sattva-bhayottaraṇāya 9. namaḥ sarva-sattva-bhaya-praçamana-karāya 10. namaḥ sarva-sattva-vyādhi-cikitsana-karāya 11. namaḥ sarva-sattva-bandhana-chedana-karāya 12. namaḥ sarva-sattva-duḥkha-pramokṣana-karāya . . . . . 57. para vidyā-saṁbhakṣaṇa-karāya . . . 59. pūja pūja 60. bhagavān hayagrīva 61. khāda khāda . . . 75. sarvaṁ grahiṣva . . . 105. kuru kuru 106. hayagrīvāya phaṭ 107. vajra-kurāya phaṭ 108. vināçaya phaṭ 109. vajra-daṁṣṭrāya phaṭ . . . 112 sarva-duṣṭa-mantraṁ vināçaya phaṭ . . . Chin.: 1—5 see page 66. 6 那麼薩婆薩埵毘+耶娑那伽底爾 7 idem 槫訶唎泥 8. id. 婆瑜跢囉那耶 9. id. 跋+囉賒麼那迦囉耶 10. id. 毘+耶地只枳瑳那迦囉耶 11. id. 盤陀那熾陀那迦囉 12. id. 獨佉波+囉木叉拏迦囉耶. . . . 57. 鉢囉比知+耶三薄叉那迦囉耶. . . 59. 部知+耶 (2×) 60. 婆伽畔何耶揭+哩婆 61. 佉陀 (2×) . . . . 75. 薩婆揭+喋醯瑟+皤 . . . 105. 句嚕 (2×) 106. 何耶揭+哩柹耶婆 107. 跋折囉齲囉耶 id. 108. 毘那賒耶 id. 109. id. 鄧瑟+吒+囉耶 id. . . . 112 id. 突瑟+吒曼跢+囉 id. id. . . . . 116 *vaḍavāmukhāya* 皤吒皤目佉耶.

12. Another great Mantra of Hayagrīva, 又馬頭別大咒.

(For the greater part a repetition of the former one)

By only chanting these two mtr. one will obtain success. Although one has not been taught the rules for altar and offerings, by only chanting them one will obtain a manifestation [1]).

13. Mantra for tying up the Vināyaka's [2]), 縛毘那夜迦咒.

If one wishes to apply these methods (given above), one should begin with tying up the Vināyaka's. Relying on the Great Mantra quoted above, one should do homage, while chanting the binding-mantra, that runs:

"Thus: scatter! scatter! Disperse, disperse! Devour, svāhā! Great Strong One! Guide to all knowledge! To the Horse-faced One! To the Bhūta! phaṭ [3])!"

This method should be practised in front of the image of Hayagrīva. One should begin with taking * * * wood [4]), cutting off a piece of eight fingers. This one should burn in the fire. Taking guggulu-perfume [5]), one should make of it (i. e. the ashes and the perfume mixed together) eight hundred pellets. These should be thrown one by one into the fire, each time saying the mtr. When all the perfume is exhausted, the Vināyaka's will be bound up on their own account.

12(a). Method for another Mantra, 又一咒法.

Doing homage as described before one should say the mtr.: * * *. This method should be used when people are suffering from *pollutiones nocturnae*. One should first say the mtr.

---

1) The text has: 波帝吒悉陀波伴底, which the commentary explains as: 唐云隨誦成驗. According to this explanation the transcribed Sanskrit-sentence might be something like: *paṭhitāraḥ siddham āpnuvanti.*

2) Cf. Hob. s. v. *Binayaka*; originally an appellation of the Hindu-god Gaṇeça, meaning: the remover of obstacles (*vighna-vināyaka, vighnajit*). The Buddhists reinterpreted this name as "he who leads away from the right path", thence: obstacle *par excellence*. Finally it stood for all evil influences that set traps for the practitioner. Here the word is used in this latter meaning.

3) *tad yathā: çru çru viçru viçru khādaya svāhā mahābala sarva-vidyā-vināyaka vaḍavāmukhine bhūtāya phaṭ*, 跢姪他主+嚕 (2×) 毘主+嚕 (2×) 伽跢耶莎訶摩訶婆羅薩婆毘知+耶毘那夜乾皤吒皤謨枯+知步跢耶抪.

4) The text has a quaint character, composed of the 140th radical on top, and then a shortened form of the 199th radical "wheat", with yü "jade" at the right side. This character is not given in K'ang-hsi-tzŭ-tien. Is it perhaps an artificial combination of two or three characters, made up according to the trick ho-tzŭ, 合字法, much practised by Mantrayānic writers, to make the text unintelligible to laymen? If so, they have succeeded well.

5) an-hsi-hsiang 安息香, Bdellion, a rare perfume; cf. Mik., p. 49.

eight-hundred times over a white thread, and then make a chaplet of it. Each time one says the mtr., one makes a knot in the cord, doing so thirty-seven times. Binding this cord round the waist one will have no *pollutiones nocturnae.*

13(a). Method for another Mantra, *idem.*

Doing homage as described before one should chant the mtr.: * * *. For applying this method one should say this mtr. over a corner of one's garment, seventeen times, and then make a knot in it. As soon as one has made this knot, the *ātmarakṣa* (cf. *supra*) will be effected.

14. Mudrā and Mantra to make Hayagrīva-Avalokiteçvara return to his own abode (i. e. at the end of the ceremony), **撥遣馬頭觀世音印咒.**

Having done homage as described before, one should say the following mtr. in order to make Hayagrīva repair to his own abode: * * *. The method is this: one should take surabhi-flowers [1]) in the hand; having once said this mtr., one should scatter the flowers over the image. When one has done this seven times, the Bs. Hayagrīva will have returned to his own abode.

(15) Rules for painting the image, **畫作像法.**

One should take a newly-made earthen pot, which has never been used before. This pot one should paint dark-blue, and on it one should paint the image of Hayagrīva-Avalokiteçvara. Its size should be one vitasti [2]) of a Tathāgata. One should give him four joyful faces. That on the left side one should paint black, with green pupils and protruding canine teeth. The face on the right side should have a flesh-colour; it is called: "Mantra-devouring face". The middle face should be a very regular-featured Bs.-face, painted white. Above the top of the image, hanging in the empty space, one should paint a dark-blue face, spitting out jewels. Each of these four heads bears a jewel-cap, and on each jewel-cap is sitting a Buddha of Transformation [3]). The left hand of the Bs. holds a lotus-flower, the arm being bent upwards so that the fist is right before the shoulder. The right hand is hanging down, with the fingers stretched out, exhibiting the "Mudrā of Expelling Fear" [4]). Both hands have jewel-bracelets at the wrists. Round the neck of the

---

1) **素羅毘布瑟波**, S. *surabhi-puṣpa*, cf. P. W., s. v.; the flower of several odoriferous plants.

2) **一搩(磔)手**, a certain measure, the exact meaning of which is not stated, cf. Mik., p. 93. The Indian *vitasti* is defined as "a long span between the thumb and little finger, or as the distance between the wrist and the tips of the fingers".

3) hua-fu **化佛.**

4) shih wu wei shou **施無畏手**, S. *abhaya-mudrā.*

image one should put precious strings of jewels. The body should be adorned according to the rules given in other places for the ornaments of Avalokiteçvara. The image is standing on a precious lotus-flower.

When ths image is finished, from the tenth day of the white moon-half[1]) on, one should eat milk-pap of rough wheat. The 13th, the 14th, and the 15th day, all these three days and nights, one should abstain from all food. Taking çākapica(?)-incense[2]) and gandha-nakuli-flowers[3]), one should chant the mantra over these two objects; each time one says the mtr. throwing them before the middle-face of the image, doing so eight-thousand times. From the mouth of this face there will come forth a large effulgence, which surrounds the body of the practitioner, and then goes back into the mouth of the image. Then this mouth will emit a Wish-granting gem[4]). If one gathers up this jewel, one will obtain a life of fourteen thousand years, becoming one of the holy Cakravartin's[5]). And after this life one will be reborn in Sukhāvatī[6]), out of the feet of Avalokiteçvara.

(16) There also is another method. One should only eat pap of milk and rough meat, given as alms, and chant the mtr. seventy thousand times. After 10 000 times the Vināyaka's are bound up. After 20 000 times all charms can be completed. After 30 000 times one can complete the method for the drug that consists of añjana and realgar[7]). Having abstained from all food during three days and three nights, one should take the medicine in one's dharma-hand. By chanting mtr.'s over the medicine, the three characteristics will manifest themselves therein: thereby one knows that the medicine is ready. The three characteristics are: heat, smoke and flames. Then one can (also) successfully perform the antardharaṇa[8]), being invisible, and become a Vidyādhara[9]), who

1) S. *çukla-pakṣa.*

2) 娑迦比遮香.

3) 乾陀那句利, cf. P. W., s. v.

4) 如意珠, *cintāmaṇi.*

5) 轉輪聖王.

6) 安樂國.

7) 安善那摩那熾羅藥. The Fan-yü-tzŭ-tien, 梵語字典 gives also 安禪 etc. The correct reading is: 安膳那, Wrightea antidysenterica, S. *añjana* (cf. Mik., p. 49). I therefore transcribe the Chin. characters as: *añjana-manaḥçila-oṣadhi.*

8) 安陀羅陀那.

9) 持咒.

has free access to the palaces of the Asura's[1]. After 40 000 times one may leave the earth and wander freely where one likes. After 50 000 times one may rise into space according to one's wish. After 60 000 times one will get a life of a thousand years. The practitioner can summon the immortals. Everything is spontaneously accomplished just as he should wish it done. He can summon all creatures he likes. After 70 000 times the hair of the practitioner will stand upright, having the shape of a conch[2], and his thoughts will carry him everywhere he likes. He is in the direct service of Avalokiteçvara, and knows of all the living beings of the three worlds: this one is going to die, this one is going to live. This is the magical success[3] one obtains.

(17) There is another method for those who want to vanquish an army[4]. During three days and three nights one should abstain from all food, remaining in front of the image of Hayagrīva, and rub the altar with incense. One should offer all kinds of flowers, clean food and drink, milk, rice-milk and all kinds of fruits. One should pound *sarjarasa*-incense[5], and knead it with white wax into eight thousand pellets. Each time one says the mtr., one should throw a pellet into the fire, doing so till all the incense is exhausted. When a throng of soldiers suddenly appears, then one is changed into a horse's head, and after a short time one is transformed into the head of Hayagrīva. When the practitioner thus miraculously approaches the soldiers, they will all be dispersed and destroyed.

(18) Another method is to give first rough wheat to a cow to eat. One selects the wheat out of the dung of this cow; when cleaned and dried one should pound it, and then cook it, making milk-pap of it. From the first day of the white moon-half till the thirteenth day, one should eat this pap. Thereupon one should abstain from all food. The ground before the image of Hayagrīva one should cover with ointment, and strew all kinds of flowers, burning all kinds of famous incense. When the offering of all kinds of food is finished, one should pound kapiça-incense[6] into powder, and knead it with water into pellets, to a number of 8000. Then one should light a fire, using khadira-wood[7]

---

1) 阿修羅.
2) 螺, *çaṅkha*.
3) cheng-chiu 成就, S. *siddhi*.
4) 西若; I transcribe these characters as S. *sainya*, though I did not find this corroborated anywhere.
5) 娑闍羅娑香, resinous exudation of the Sāla-tree, cf. Buk, p. 600.
6) 迦比闍香.
7) 迦地羅木, acacia catechu, cf. Mik. 284.

as fuel. Each time taking one incense-pellet, one should throw it into the fire, each time saying the mtr. When in this way the eight thousand pellets are used up, the remaining ashes will be found to have altered into a piece of gold [1]), weighing 100 000 pound.

(19) Another method for destroying the spells said by other people. One should take a little of one's own blood, and knead it with white mustard-seed into eight thousand pellets. On the fourteenth day of the black moonhalf [2]), one should abstain from food during the whole day, and light a fire in a furnace, using khadira-wood as fuel. Taking the mustard-seed pellets mentioned above, one should throw them into the fire and burn them, each time chanting the mtr. When in this way all the mustard-seed pellets are used up, all kinds of spells will be destroyed [3]) completely.

(20) There is also a method, consisting of only chanting the mtr. When one travels through a wilderness or over a sandy plain, the food one should need will appear on its own account.

(21) There is also a method for when there is a sun- or moon-eclipse. One should take two new earthen bowls, filled with pure ghee. Holding these bowls in one's hands, one should look up to the sun or the moon. Having chanted the mtr. over the ghee in these bowls, it will grow warm, and sometimes smoke and fire will come out of it. When at the same time one drinks this ghee or applies it to one's body, then one has only to think of a place, and one is already there. If one keeps continually chanting this mtr., all one's fears will be annihilated, and all obstacles and difficulties will vanish.

(22) There is also a method in case one is suffering from ruddha-wounds [4]), or in case one is bitten by venomous snakes, or one is suffering from * * * -wounds [5]). For all these wounds one should one thousand times chant the mtr. over yellow mud. If one applies this mud on the wounds, they will disappear. All anxiousness and fear will disappear too.

(23) There is also a method in case one should be in danger on the water. If one says (this mtr.) in his heart, one will not be drowned.

(24) All these methods should not be told to other people. Then they will succeed

---

1) 蘇跋那, S. *suvarṇa*.
2) S. *kṛṣṇa-pakṣa*.
3) The text has: 喫, explained as a word from a foreign language (Mongolian?), meaning: to destroy.
4) 路陀 (?)
5) 健毘吒鷄 (?).

according to one's desire. When one makes a large maṇḍala, one may not use it to obtain foolish desires.

(25) Rules for making an image of Hayagrīva, 作何耶揭唎婆像法.

Again there is another method for making an image. One should take a piece of clean cloth, that may not be cut off. One engages a painter of the greatest skill, without haggling over the price. One should bathe in perfumed water, put on new, clean clothes, observe the eight precepts, and do so day by day. On a pure and clean place one should erect a "water-altar", four cubits square. The practitioner, having finished the ātmarakṣa and the marking off the place, should burn on this altar all kinds of incense, and strew all kinds of flowers. When the offering is finished, one should on this altar put the painted Bs., having the size of one vitasti of a Buddha. He has four faces in all. The middle-face of the Bs. should be made very regular-featured, expressing compassion. It has a light flesh-colour, while the hair on the head is of a pure dark-blue colour. The face on the left side one should make having a very angry look, and having a black colour. It has protruding canine teeth. The hair on this head is standing up loosely, having the colour of flames. The face on the right side one should give a broadly laughing expression; it has a light flesh-colour, and is regular like the face of a Bs. The hair on this head is of a pure dark-blue colour. Each of this three heads carries a heaven-cap, and ear-ornaments of jade. On each heaven-cap there is a Buddha of Transformation, sitting cross-legged. On top of the middle-head one should paint a green-blue horse's head, with its mouth shut [1]. Round the neck of the Bs. one should put a beautiful necklace, and behind his back one should make a halo of different colours. The left hand, bent to the breast, holds a red lotus-flower. This lotus-flower should be on one level with the head of the Bs., and near the left shoulder. On the platform consisting of this flower, one should paint a Buddha of Transformation, clad in a red-brown garment [2], and sitting cross-legged. Behind his back there is a halo. The right hand has an uplifted palm, with the five fingers stretched out. The arm is evenly bent, and on the palm of the hand it carries a Wish-granting Gem. This round jewel is white, and it is surrounded by a flesh-coloured halo. In this right hand, exactly under the jewel, there is a shower of all kinds of jewels. Over the right shoulder he wears a tiger-skin [3], put on in the same way as a saṁkakṣika-garment [4]. Under the right

---

1) It is to be noted that the horse's head is counted as a face of the god (cf. also sub. 15), contrary to the Indian custom.

2) 袈裟, S. *kāṣāya*.

3) 弊耶迦羅者摩, S. *vyāghra-carman*.

4) 僧祇支, cf. Buk., page 1072.

arm-pit this covering skin is fastened with a knot. A tiger-skin is used also to cover the thighs. Besides (the ornaments mentioned here) the bracelets, the heavenly gown[1]) etc., are all according to the general rules for painting a Bs. If one makes the Bs. sit erect on a red lotus-flower, then there should in the empty place above him hang the precious parasol, covering the head of the Bs. In the empty space above one should paint all kinds of heavenly musical instruments, and in the empty space on both sides one should paint Çuddhāvāsa-gods[2]), dancing and offering. While painting this image one should mix the colours with perfumed sap, and not with glue.

(26) Altar for the initiation to the cult of the Bs. Hayagrīva Avalokiteçvara, **馬頭觀世音菩薩受法壇**.

If there is a çramaṇa or a brāhmaṇa, or a good man or woman, who wants to be taught the rules for the cult of this Bs., one should make an altar of four cubits square, as described above (see sub 7). One should choose an excellent place, that has been cleaned and washed with water. Then one should smear the earth with perfumed water and cow-dung. One should hang there all kinds of coloured banners, baldaquins, precious bells and jade mirrors. The bodhimaṇḍa should be adorned with all kinds of gold and silver. In the middle of this bodhimaṇḍa a five-coloured altar should be erected, four cubits square. First one should paint the white colour, then the yellow, then the red, then the blue and finally the black. One should make there four gates. Right in the middle of the altar one should make a lotus-seat, and thereon one should put the image of Hayagrīva. In front of the eastern gate one should make a lotus-seat, on which the Bodhisattva-with-eleven-faces is seated. Before the northern gate one should make a lotus-seat, and place thereon the Eight-armed Avalokiteçvara. At the southern side of the altar there is no need to put a lotus-seat. There one should place the eight Dragon-Kings[3]). In which order should these eight be placed? The first is Nanda, the second Vāsuki, the third Takṣaka, the fourth Karkoṭaka, the fifth Padma, the sixth Mahāpadma, the seventh Çaṅkhapāla, the eight Kulika[4]). To these eight Dragon-Kings one should only offer dry rice and milk-pap. To the other deities one should offer all kinds of drink and food. Also

---

1) t'ien-i-ch'ün 天衣裙, feather-light garments of the gods.

2) 須陀會天; I am not sure my transcription is right.

3) 龍王, S. *nāga-rāja*.

4) 難陀、婆素雞、德叉迦、羯固吒、般摩、摩訶 id., 商佉波羅、鳩利迦.

one should light forty-five lamps. One should begin with calling the eight Dragon-Kings to occupy their places, using the mtr. of the body of the Bs. Hayagrīva [1]), saying the mtr.: * * *.

(27) At the southern side of the altar one should place a brazier. Then one should take linseed, rice and flowers, and mix these with honey. One should chant the mtr. of the Heart of the Bs. [2]). The things one has mixed together before saying the mtr., one should throw now in the fire, each time one chants the mtr. When one has done this 1008 times, one should bid the Bs. Hayagrīva who dwells in the heart to come. Thereupon one should bid the Eight-armed Bs. Avalokiteçvara on the northern side to come. Making the mdr. of the Body of the Bs. [3]), moving the fingers to and fro, one should chant the mtr.: * * *.

(28) Thereupon one should bid the Bs.-with-eleven-faces on the eastern side to come, using the mdr. of the lotus-seat. Having installed the seat, one should strew all kinds of flowers, and burn all kinds of famous incense. One should offer agaru [4]), kunduruka- [5]) and sandal-perfume. The practitioner should during one day abstain from all food. If he can not stand the hunger, he may eat soup made of perfumed ghee. Then he should bathe himself, and put on new clothes. He should enter the maṇḍala and bring offerings. He should constantly think of the Bs. Avalokiteçvara. Then one will get all siddhi's and manifestations of all Bs. If one wants to have a dispute, one should make an altar of this kind, and make offerings on it. Then one will always win, and not be pressed hard by other people. One even can drive others into a corner. If an illness is hard to be cured, one has only to make this altar: then all diseases will vanish. If one is injured by poison or venomous insects or by a tiger, one only has to chant this mtr., and one will be cured.

(29) One should pound (dried) sumukha-plants [6]) into very fine powder, and mix it with koumiss [7]), in the same way as one would mix rice-pap. Hereover one should chant thirty-seven times the mtr. of the Heart of Hayagrīva-Avalokiteçvara. If one gives this pap to the sick person when he has an empty stomach, he will spit out all venomous insects that are there.

---

1) See sub 2. 2) See sub 3. 3) See sub 2.

4) 沈水, cf. Mik. page 12.

5) 薰陸, cf. Mik., p. 427.

6) 酥木佉子; S. *sumukha* indicates various plants, i.a. ocimum basillicum pilosum. The Fan-yü-tzŭ-tien explains these characters as meaning hiṅgu.

7) 酪.

CHAPTER IV

HAYAGRĪVA IN JAPAN

1. Horse-cult before the Introduction of Buddhism

In Japan the horse is mentioned as occurring already in the mythological age.

When the Food-goddess Uke-mochi-no-kami 保食神 offers unclean food to the Moon-god, his anger is roused, and he slays her. Then it appears that "on the crown of her head there had been produced the ox and the horse; on the top of her forehead there had been produced millet; over her eyebrows there had been produced the silk-worm" [1]).

Furthermore we find the horse in the ancient myth concerning the Sun-goddess and her fierce brother Susa-no-o. Susa-no-o breaks the dikes of the rice-fields that had been laid out by his sister, and concludes his crimes by "flaying a piebald horse with a backward flaying", and throwing this into the sacred hall, where his sister is weaving. Being frightened she inflicts a bleeding wound upon herself with the spool; indignant at this outrage she hides herself in a chasm.

I will not make an attempt to explain this motif in a phallic sense, neither will I endeavour to prove that this story is a remnant of an ancient incest-myth, although this theory seems very probable, if we may consider this motif in the light of later Japanese popular beliefs.

In popular belief the horse is closely connected with the idea of fecundity, and plays as such, a very important rôle in sexual life. This may be explained by the fact that phallicism is very popular in Japan; the well-known works on Shintō give ample information concerning this matter [2]). The Japanese word for horse, uma, accordingly has various sexual meanings. In the first place uma is a nickname for a prostitute, for obvious reasons; furthermore it means a powerful membrum virile, and finally it is a street-word for the menses [3]). In all these significations it has found its way into popular poetry. In my opinion at the base of these associations lies the ancient conception which

1) Aston, Nihongi, Chronicles of Japan from the earliest times to A.D. 697, London 1896, I, p. 33.

2) Cf. Aston, Shintō, the Way of the Gods, London 1905, p. 186—198; Nachod, Geschichte von Japan, Gotha 1906, I, p. 122—155; Satow und Ihm, Japanisches Geschlechtsleben, Leipzig 1931, index, s.v. Phallicism.

3) Satow u. Ihm, op cit., II, p. 347; 301, 326, 344, 430; 345.

connects the horse, via phallicism, with fecundity. So the motif of Susa-no-o outraging his sister could be interpreted, if we take the horse as a phallic symbol, as a disguised account of the fact that he violated his sister; after this pollution she hides herself in the rock.

We see the horse also playing an important rôle in Japanese marriage-customs. Most of the marriages are contracted in the evening; the marriage of a daimyō, however, is contracted in the day-time, between eleven and one, the hour of the horse. See further also WATANABE, Marriage customs in Japan, Yokohama, 1894, page 23 and 30.

These motifs are purely Japanese; with regard to horses as sacrificial gifts, however, the problem is more complicated. In this connection the Chinese custom of presenting horses to accompany the dead into the grave (cf. *supra*, page 42, 43) has probably been of influence. It seems that this custom was imitated on a large scale in Japan; for in the Taikwa Reform (645—650) this custom is disapproved of [1]).

I do not venture to conclude whether, and to what extent, this custom is connected with the presenting of horses to Shintō-temples. For these offerings preferably white horses were chosen; they were led into an enclosure near the temple, where they could walk about freely [2]). Also with these horses the sexual element is traceable: the sacred horse functions as a scape-goat for adulterous women. On the sixteenth of June in the Usaka-jinja, the Shintō-temple of Usakamura, Fukigun, Toyamaken, the Shimotodachi-festival is celebrated. Women, who in the past year have committed adultery, confess this to the priest, and their sin is redeemed by the sacred horse being beaten. Formerly the women themselves had to undergo this punishment [3]).

The Japanese votive pictures, ema 繪馬 seem to be a remnant of these horse-offerings to temples. Originally these ema were, as may be derived from the name, images of horses.

According to the Kansōzuihitsu 閑窓隨筆, in 1825 edited by T. SUZUKI [4]), these ema originated from the custom of presenting live horses as offerings. Those people who could not afford such large presents gave wooden horses, and those who had no money for even these presents, gave images of horses. Later on pictures of horses were not exclusively given, but also various sorts of other paintings, or even simple tablets

1) NACHOD, op. cit., I, page 311.

2) ASTON, Shintō, p. 221.

3) SATOW u. IHM, op. cit., II, page 79.

4) Cf. Daihyakkajiten 大百科事典, Heibonsha-edition, 1934, s. v. *ema*.

with some verses pencilled on them. According to this source sexual images predominated. It seems, however, that the authorities took action against this. The origin of this practice lies, in my opinion, in the wide-spread belief that sexual representations ward off all sorts of calamities [1]); the ema, being originally pictures of horses, were very suitable for this.

The Honchōmonsui 本朝文粋, in the 11th century written by Fujiwara Akihira [2]), carries the sacrificing of images of horses back to Oe Tadahira, who in 1012 was the first to offer some images of horses, painted on coloured paper.

With regard to these ema I think that the Buddhist idea of tne divine horse, which transmits the prayers of men to the gods (see *supra*, page 46) also contributed to the development of this usage. As in Japan, however, Shintō and Buddhism are so strongly mixed, this is difficult to ascertain.

In popular Japanese religion the ema obtained the signification of a thank-offering: a seaman, safely returned from a dangerous voyage, presents a picture of a ship at sea. The ema are also given as token of a vow that has been made: a drunkard, who turns over a new leaf, offers a picture of a sake-bowl, fitted with a large lock; a gambler gives a picture of a man cleaving some dice with an axe [3]). The inscription on an ema is usually nothing more than hōnō 奉納 "presented"; frequently also the date is mentioned. It is not allowed to mention the name of the giver; as a rule only the year of his birth is quoted, for instance "offered by a man born in the year of the sheep". Often the whole ema is nothing more than a picture of the cyclic animal, indicating the birth-year of the giver. Finally some ema represent the substitute of the gift which one would have offered, if one's means had permitted; to this category belong images of cows, purses, pieces of gold etc.

The huge quantities of these votive pictures that were presented to temples, Buddhist as well as Shintō, necessitated the adding of a special hall to the temple, called emadō 繪馬堂. The ema-collections of the Kiyomizu-temple 清水 in Kyōto, the Hatsu-

---

1) Cf. ASTON, Shintō, p. 186, 187; WALEY, Magical use of phallic representations, its late survival in Chine and Japan, Bull. Museum of Far-Eastern Antiquities, III, Stockholm 1931, p. 61. A similar beliet exists in India: S. LÉVI, Le Nepal, II, p. 21 speaks about sexual representations on the walls of temples: "L'explication que j'en ai recueillie est uniforme: ces scènes passent pour avoir la vertu d'écarter la foudre".

2) Cf. KOKUSHI, s. v. *ema*.

3) These examples are taken from the interesting booklet "Ema, the votive pictures of Japan", by J. H. DE FOREST, 1914, where many illustrations are given; cf. also the illustrations by the article *ema*, in Daihyakkajiten.

segawa-temple 初瀬 in the old province of Yamato, and the Itsukushima-嚴島 temple in Aki[1]) have a well-merited fame[2]). Often this hall has kept the character of a stable; for instance at the great temple in Izumo, the Umaya, "stable", where in 1666 a bronze horse was placed[3]). Compare also the bronze horse in the Shintō-temple of Suwa, at Nagasaki[4]).

From the above-mentioned data it is evident that in Japan the horse was intimately connected with the conception of fecundity, and as such gained great popularity in the religion of the people.

In the following chapter we shall see that the figure of Hayagrīva was readily linked up with these conceptions.

2. The Buddhist Hayagrīva

In Japan the Chinese Mantrayāna was systematized further and rounded off to one of the twelve great Japanese Buddhist secs, under the name of Shingon-shū 眞言宗, the Mantra-sect. The Japanese patriarch of this sect is the famous priest Kōbō Daishi 弘法大師 (Kūkai 空海, 774—835); in 804 he set out for China, and became there a pupil of the seventh patriarch of the Chinese Mantrayāna, Hui Kuo (see *supra*, page 25). Kōbō Daishi transmitted the Doctrine to his pupils Jitsu-e 實慧, 786—847) and Shin-ga (眞雅, 801—879).

It is not necessary to give here a detailed description of the tenets of the Shingon-sect[5]). Generally speaking, they are an enlarged copy of the Chinese system, the pivot being formed by the Magic Circle of the Two Sections (ryōbu 兩部): the Vajradhātu (Kongōkai 金剛界), the noumenal, and the Garbhadhātu (Taizōkai 胎藏界), the phenomenal aspect of the world. Here also the figure of Hayagrīva must be looked for in the third section of the Garbhadhātu, the Lotus-section (Rengge-bu 華部蓮), after the central figure Avalokiteçvara also called Kannonin 觀音院. In this section Hayagrīva occupies the seventh place in the first row. See the picture of the Taizōkai, in Him., facing page 718. In Japan Hayagrīva bears all his Chinese titles, like Dairijimyōō

---

1) Cf. Daihyakkajiten, s. v. *ema*.

2) In 1832 a catalogue of this collection was published, the Itsukushima-ema-kagami (WEBER, Ko-ji-hō-ten, Paris 1923, s. v. *ema*).

3) Cf. SCHURHAMMER, Shintō, Bonn 1923, p. 175; on page 149 a picture of the emadō of Kitano, Kyōto is given. The Leyden Museum possesses a beautiful model of an emadō at Ōsaka, 1146/1.

4) Cf. F. CHAILAYE, Le Japon, Paris 1915, page 117.

5) For a good summary see H. SCHMIDT, Eine populäre Darstellung der Shingon Lehre, Ostasiatische Zeitschrift, 1918, p. 45, 1920, p. 103.

大力持明王, etc.; usually, however, he is called Batō-kannon (馬頭觀音, seldom Mezukannon). Cf. Chinese names on page 47, *supra*.

Just as in Tibet and Mongolia (see *supra*, p. 28), Batōkannon is in Japanese popular religion considered as a protector of horses and cattle in general. As such he is identified with one of the Six Kannons of the Tendai-sect, Shishimuikanzeon 師子無畏觀世音. His statues are to be found all along the country-roads, and special temples are devoted to him [1]). The most famous are the Entsūji 圓通寺, at the foot of Mount Fuji, where formerly in September horse-races were held in his honour; and the Matsuodera 松尾寺 in the Tango-province, where he in his female aspect is venerated as one of the 33 Kannons of the West. In the Kannon-temple at Komatsubara, Futakawa, Mikawa-province, in the second month the people offer wooden *ema*, with representations of animals, cows, horses etc. to the image of Batō [2]).

The Shingon and Tendai-sects show a strong syncretic tendency; Shingon especially took over many Shintō-elements. One of the first Shintō-gods that was incorporated in Shingon is the famous war-god Hachiman, who in 783 was received in the ranks of the Bodhisattva's. We saw in the first part of this chapter, that the horse in its quality ot fecundity-symbol occupied a prominent place in Shintō. In my opinion it is because of this association that Batōkannon became a God of the Roads. In Japan there exists a very old cult of phallic gods of the roads, as for instance the God of the Cross-ways Kunadō 岐神, and others [3]). The countless images of Hayagrīva standing alongside the roads are essentially so many phalli, that by their decent shape did not offend the eye of the authorities. This is most apparent in those cases, where one finds a simple stone, bearing the name of Batōkannon.

In Japanese iconography Hayagrīva is represented in all the various forms that are described or hinted at in the different passages of the Canon, quoted in the former chapter. Some, however, are made according to the directions to be found in the special text, in Japan devoted to Hayagrīva, which I will discuss below. Although these representations are copied from Chinese originals (that go back on Indian prototypes), yet many of these images, especially those in bronze, show a typical Japanese style. Compare, e. g., the bronze statue of the Kanzeonji (Hob. I, Plate VII), and the painting of the Boston Museum of Fine Arts (reproduced in Kokka, No. 385, June 1922).

---

1) Cf. the article Batōkannon, in Hob., page 60.

2) Cf. Nihonminzokujiten, by T. Nakayama, Tōkyō 1933, s. v. *ema*.

3) Cf. Aston, Shinto, page 187, 189; Kokushi 815.

X. Hayagrīva as represented in the Taizōkai.

XI. Hayagrīva sitting on a rock (Ts. P. S., part III, No. 56)

The Picture Section of Ts. (大像經圖像) gives many images of Hayagrīva, taken from manuscripts preserved in various Japanese monasteries. The text of these documents is also to be found reprinted there. These texts contain lengthy discussions of the Canonical passages regarding Hayagrīva, often in the form of a conversation between teacher and pupil. I have selected here four pictures, which may serve to illustrate the Japanese texts, as well as the Chinese descriptive passages, translated *supra*, Ch. III, sub C and D.

3. Hayagrīva in the Japanese Canon

The Taishō Issaikyō contains all the scriptures that are used in Japanese Buddhism. They are all written in the Chinese language; this fact, however, does not imply that they originate from China.

The works of the Shingon-sect are collected in Ts. XVIII, XIX, XX and XXI. Here one finds, next to the fundamental texts, translated by famous teachers like Vajrabodhi, Amoghavajra etc. from Sanskrit into Chinese, also a large number of longer and shorter texts, the source of which is difficult to determine. They are often compounded like a mosaic-pattern from fragments of these basic texts, scraps out of non-canonical documents, together with many repetitions. The same detailed description of the ritual with which a certain deity must be worshipped (i-kuei 儀軌, Jap. giki, S. *kalpa*) will often be found repeated in exactly the same terms in a text which is dedicated to quite another deity. It would be incorrect to speak here of plagiarism or falsification, especially in those cases where the gods concerned belong to the same family (S. *kula*), or in another manner could be classified in one and the same group. It goes without saying that the ritual with which Akṣobhya is worshipped, can just as well be used for his spiritual son Vajrapāṇi, and for his emanation Vajrasattva. But even if such a group-connection is lacking, then the use of the same text for the worship of different gods is justified by the fact that all gods are identical as manifestations of the Void (S. *çūnyatā*).

When fragments from longer texts are detached and combined in a separate entirety, dedicated to a certain deity, then this must be considered as a special mark of distinction paid to that god.

An example of such a case may be found in the long text which is especially dedicated to Hayagrīva in the Japanese Canon. The title of this text (Ts. 1072 A) runs: "Methods and Rules for Incantations and Offerings to effect a manifestation of the Great Fierce King, the Holy Hayagrīva" (Shōkayakiribadaiinuō ryūjō daishinken kuyōnenju gikihōbon, 聖賀野紇哩縛大威怒王立成大神驗供養念誦儀軌法品). This is the most important text used in Japan for the worship of Hayagrīva. The Ts.-redaction is based on three texts, respectively dated: Kyōhō-period 享保, 1716—1735; the sixth year of the Kyū-an-period 久安, i. e. 1150, and the eighth year of the period Kuạnji 寛治, i. e. 1094. This text, which is divided into two chapters, is said to have been translated by Imperial command by Amoghavajra, who is mentioned with all his titles and distinctions. This fact, however, does not prove the authenticity of the text; the fame of Amoghavajra was so great, that his name was often made use of to give more authority to a text by its presence. Hence the mention of Amoghavajra did not prevent the priest Jōgon (淨嚴, 1639—1702) from doubting the genuineness of this text.

On minute analysis this text appears to consist of various fragments, that form an artificial whole.

After some introductory verses, the text commences with the beginning of another kalpa, viz. Ts. 1056, "Rules to be practised for the Bs. Avalokiteçvara-with-thousand-eyes-and-hands, according to the Vajraçekhara-sūtra" (Chin-kang-ting-yu-ch'ieh ch'ien-shou-ch'ien-yen kuan-tzŭ-tsai-p'u-sa hsiu-hsing i-kuei ching 金剛頂瑜伽千手千眼觀自在菩薩修行儀軌經). This is a genuine Chinese text, mentioned in the Cheng-yüan-hsin-ting-shih-chiao-mu-lu (see *supra*, page 57), page 879. Ts. 1072 A, on the contrary, is not mentioned in any Chinese catalogue. Chapter I of our text is further wholly composed of shorter and longer citations from Ts. 1056, alternated by fragments which mostly have nothing at all to do with Hayagrīva. Then on page 159—160 a detailed description is given of the ritual which one should perform in order to call up Hayagrīva in one's soul, and to behold him in the centre of his Maṇḍala, his Magic Circle. Now this passage forms the kernel, as it were, round which the whole text is grouped. For the text that precedes it, although composed from very heterogeneous elements, yet does not lack a certain unity: the leading thought is to describe a series of introductory rites, which are required for preparing the body and soul of the practitioner. When these rites are performed one will by the inspection of various mystic syllables (*bīja*) be able to behold the god. It goes without saying that for the compilation of this text one made use of a text devoted to Avalokiteçvara, as Hayagrīva is a special aspect of this Bs.

The second chapter is an elaboration of the Maṇḍala of Hayagrīva. The various figures that form part of this maṇḍala are here again each dealt with in detail, together

XII. Hayagrīva with Staff and Lotus-flower. (Ts. P. S., part IV, No. 1)

XIII. Hayagrīva on the water-buffalo. (Ts. P. S., part III, No. 71)

with a precise description of their respective mdr. and mtr. All these figures having been discussed at length, the remaining part of this second chapter consists of a collection of fragments, for the greater part borrowed from Chapter VI of the Dhāraṇī-saṁgraha, alternated by short, independent passages. One of these, the description of Hayagrīva sitting on a water-buffalo (page 168) has been taken from a text that is especially devoted to another Vidyārāja, viz. Yamāntaka (Ts. 1214: Sheng-yen-man-te-chia-wei-nu-wang li-ch'eng ta-shen-yen nien-sung-fa 聖閻曼德迦威怒王立成大神驗念誦法, an authentic Chinese text). The last part of this second chapter, finally, is a synthesis of all passages regarding Hayagrīva, scattered over other texts of the Canon. In ch. III, section D, I have already translated these shorter references.

This special Hayagrīva-text is thus built up out of three authentic texts of the Chinese Canon:

A. Ts. 1056, devoted to the Bs. Avalokiteçvara-with-thousand-eyes-and-hands; this text is mentioned in a Chinese Catalogue, dating from the 8th century.

B. Ts. 901, the Dhāraṇī-saṁgraha, translated in 653.

C. Ts. 1214, devoted to Yamāntaka; this text existed in China during the Ming-dynasty (Nanjō's Catalogue, No. 1422).

As this compilation does not occur in any Chinese Catalogue, we may conclude that this Hayagrīva-text is a later Japanese production, written in honour of the god Hayagrīva. One need not be astonished that it was in Japan that this text was compiled; for as we saw above, in Japan horse and horse-cult occupied an important place. The figure of Hayagrīva was linked up with these conceptions, and thereby gained greater importance. On account of this promotion a special text was compiled which united all the material concerning him that was available in the Canon, into one extensive ritual, grouped round a description of his special Magic Circle.

There remain, however, those passages that deal especially with Hayagrīva, and which are not borrowed from A, B or C. These passages do not occur in other texts of the Canon, for else they would have been registrated by the priests who compiled the special accounts of Hayagrīva, published in the different parts of Ts. Picture Section. It is difficult to trace their origin. From their contents it appears clearly that they could not have been written in Japan, for the general social conditions alluded to are typically Chinese. I quote, for instance, a passage on page 168: "...if all kinds of calamities and disasters should arise, and when the land would be in disorder, when resentful enemies in other countries plot an invasion, and make several attacks; when the people are discontented, and the ministers plan rebellion; when epidemics harass the land, when there are floods and droughts, and when the regular course of sun and moon is broken..." (若種種災難起國土亂、他國怨敵數來侵擾、百姓不安大臣謀叛、疾流行水旱不調日月失度). These lines might refer to Chinese or also Indian conditions, but they can not be applied to Japan. This and similar passages could be fragments of a special Chinese Hayagrīva-text, that was lost at an early date. This, however, does not seem very probable. In my opinion they are remnants of sādhana's and short rituals, that have been transmitted in fragments, outside the Canon.

The remaining fragments, that have no special bearing upon Hayagrīva, are probably to be found hidden somewhere in the Canon.

Finally the Japanese Canon contains three brief texts, that are devoted to Hayagrīva.

Ts. 1073, Kayakiribazōhō 何耶揭唎婆像法 is a fragment of Chapter VI of the Dhāraṇī-saṁgraha, and so is also Ts. 1074 Kayakiribakanzeombosatsujuhōdan, id. 觀世音菩薩受法壇.

Ts. 1072B, Batōkannonshindarani 馬頭觀音心陀羅尼 is a brief text, written in Siddhaṁ-characters. I reproduce this text below, with a transcription. As it seems very corrupt, I have made no attempt to correct the Sanskrit.

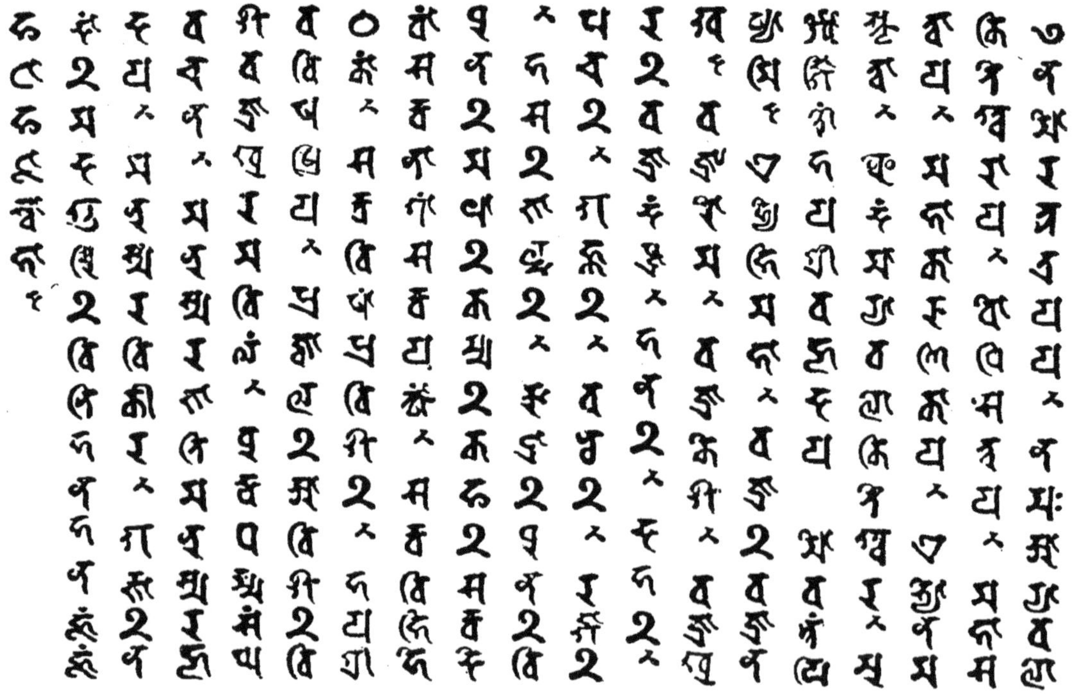

XIV. Batōkannonshindarani.

oṁ namo ratnatrayaya namaḥ āryāvalokiteçvarāya bodhisatvaya mahāsatvāya mahākaruṇikāya ebhyo namaskṛtvā idam āryāvalokiteçvara mu * * *hayagrīvahṛdaya... movantaṁ yiṣyāmi ehyehi mahāvajra vajranakha vajraroma vajrakeça vajrakhura vajradaṁṣṭra hana daha paca gahṇa bandha raṅga hasa jalda ṛtra dhuna vidhuna mathā kasya kapha sarvadevāṁ sarvanāgāṁ sarvayakṣāṁ sarvavihiheṭhakāṁ sarvaviṣāṁ praviça hayagrīva viṣaṣriya prajvāla āviça viçavajrakhuramavilaṁ buddhadharmasaṁghavacana manusyarajati manusyarahṛdaya manusyara vikīra garja nadāṁ madagu * * vinihana hana hūṁ hūṁ phaṭ phaṭ ū svāhā.

ANALYSIS

OF "METHODS AND RULES FOR INCANTATIONS AND OFFERINGS TO EFFECT A MANIFESTATION OF THE GREAT FIERCE KING, THE HOLY HAYAGRĪVA"

FIRST CHAPTER

The text opens with the following introductory verses of a general nature; the name Hayagrīva occurs once.

"Hail to Vajrapāṇi 1), the great Bodhisattva, the Lord of Mystery 2), who can explain the highest Vehicle, and make one quickly realize 3) the Enlightenment 4). To Hayagrīva 5), who can remove all obstacles of Māra 6), who, manifesting a fierce appearance, by this contradictory means 7) yet shows his compassion. Who transforms himself into the great, awe-inspiring sun-disk, which illuminates the innumerable worlds, in the same way as the darkness of the practitioners of the Yoga-doctrine 8), to whom he shows the ways of quickly obtaining magical success 9). Who abundantly sheds ambrosia 10), washing away the

1) Chin-kang-shou 金剛手. 2) Mi-chu 密主.
3) cheng 證, realize by intuition, S. *abhisameti.*
4) 菩提, S. *bodhi.* 5) 賀野紇哩縛.
6) mo-chang 魔障. 7) fang-pien 方便, S. *upāya.*
8) hsiu-hsing-che 修行者. 9) hsi-ti 悉地, S. *siddhi.*
10) kan-lou-shui 甘露水, S. *amṛta.*

memory-seeds [1]) in the All-conserving-mind [2]); who quickly effects the accumulation of pure knowledge [3]), completing the pure Essential Body. To whom I therefore do homage with my head bowed to the ground.

Now I will explain the most secret Ritual, relying on the secret tradition and the mysterious Naya-doctrine [4]).

The Teacher [5]) should begin by choosing a pupil, who wishes to practise the Mantrayāna [6]), and who has a pure faith in the Three Jewels. Who reverently loves the Great Vehicle, and thirsting looks up to the Yoga-doctrine [7]). Who can practise well the conduct of a Bodhisattva, and in whose heart there is no fear. Who will, in the search for the Yoga-doctrine, abandon his life and his earthly goods. Who is never wearied and ever compassionate, and whose family is provided with all stocks of merit [8]). Who has a profound erudition, who protects the Right Doctrine [9]), who loves and takes pleasure in the practice of the six Virtues of Perfection [10]); whose thoughts are full of compassion for all living creatures, and who constantly is covered by the armour of the Great Vow [11]). Who saves without exception all the living creatures of the innumerable worlds, and makes them quickly realize the Enlightenment.

When the Teacher sees that the pupil is a man suitable to be made an instrument of the Law [12]), he urges him on with all means, beginning by explaining to him the mysterious Path to Enlightenment [13]), the subtle Practice of Knowledge [14]) in order to quickly reach the road that leads to Buddhahood [15]); the acceptance of the Threefold Refuge [16]),

---

1) hsün-hsi-chung-tzŭ 薰習種子, S. *vāsana-bīja*: "Every act, mental and physical, leaves its seed behind, which is planted in the Ālaya for future germination under favourable conditions" (D. T. Suzuki, Studies in the Laṅkāvatāra Sūtra, London 1930, p. 438. In the following I shall often quote the sharp definitions, given in the Sanskrit-Chinese-English Glossary, which the author has added to this admirable book).

2) tsang-shih 藏識, S. *ālaya-vijñāna*.

3) fu-chih-chü 福智聚, S. *puṇya-jñāna-sambhāra*.

4) Li-ch'ü-chiao 理趣教.

5) a-che-li 阿闍梨, S. *ācārya*.

6) hsiu-mi-yen-ti-tzu 修密言弟子.

7) hsiang-ying-men 相應門.

8) chu-ken 諸根, S. *kuçala-mūla*.

9) cheng-fa 正法, S. *saddharma*.

10) liu-tu 六度, S. *pāramitā*.

11) ta-shih 大誓, S. *mahāpraṇidhāna*.

12) fa-ch'i 法器.

13) 菩提道.

14) pan-jo-li 般若理, S. *prajñā-naya*.

15) 菩提路.

16) san-kuei 三歸, S. *triçaraṇa*.

and he makes him develop the Bodhi-mind [1]. Then he teaches him the removal of all obstacles in past, present and future [2], the Threefold Morality [3], and the discipline of a Bodhisattva. Then he makes him enter the Round Altar [4]. He informs him about the personal deity [5], and by chanting magic formulae he protects the inaugural ceremony of the Anointment [6]. He should teach him to draw the Magic Circle [7], and inform him on the special discipline to be followed when adoring this deity [8]: "From now on until you become a Buddha, do not abandon the Bodhi-mind. Worship your Teacher, and try to equal all the Buddhas. Keep firm to the Vajra. Be deeply reverent and abstain from haughtiness with regard to all other esoteric schools".

From the Teacher (the pupil) now receives the Vajra, and also the Vajra-stone [9], to search with these the ways to magical success. Till he comes to the Bodhimaṇḍa [10], he should keep to these rules without ever abandoning them. Approaching with love the Teacher who grants him the Anointment [11], he should receive the discipline regarding the personal deity, resolutely, without doubt or errors, and then courageously go on to the practice".

Page 155, *b* 15—25; these lines are with some slight alterations taken from Ts. 1056, where they occur on page 72, *a* 14—23.

---

1) 菩提心, S. *Bodhicitta*. 2) san-shih 三世, S. *tryadhvan*.

3) san-chung-chieh 三種戒, S. *çīla*. *Çila* consists of strict observance of the san-men 三門 or san-yeh 三業 (S. *trividha-dvāra*), i. e. purity of body, speech and thought.

4) lun-t'an 輪壇, the same as the Great Maṇḍala, cf. Mik., p. 2290.

5) pen-tsun 本尊; it is difficult to find an exact translation of this term. The Sanskrit transcription runs 娑也地提嚩多, which seems to suggest a word like *sayādhi-devatā* (cf. Mik, p. 2068). By some European writers it is translated by *iṣṭadevatā*.

6) kuan-ting 灌頂, S. *abhiṣeka*, cf. Mik., p. 409.

7) 曼荼羅, S. *maṇḍala*, cf. Mik. 2095. 8) 三昧耶, S. *samaya*.

9) chin-kang-ch'ing 金剛磬, a Buddhist cult-object consisting of a sonorous stone, hung up in a frame and struck like a bell. The ch'ing is a Chinese musical instrument. In India it was not known, but the appellation chien-chih 犍稚, S. *gaṇḍī*, points to a similar Indian instrument, made of wood, and struck with a wooden hammer (S. *koṭanaka*). Cf., however, the extensive discussion in the Fan-i Ming-i Chi 翻譯名義集, ch. VII, sub 60, where chien-chih is translated as chung 鐘, bell. See further Mik., p. 257, 435 and 428, where a picture of the ch'ing is given, and Stael-Holstein, Gaṇḍīstotragāthā (Bibl. Buddhica XV), p. XXI, with picture of a *gaṇḍī*.

10) 菩提場, cf. Mik., p. 1660. 11) Kuan-ting-shih 灌頂師.

Page 155, *b* 25—*c* 25 seem to have been borrowed from a text devoted to another Fierce King. They contain, however, some references to Hayagrīva.

Page 155, *c* 26—page 156 *c* 21 are all taken from Ts. 1056, where they may be found on page 72, *a* 23—page 73, *b* 2.

Page 156, *c* 22—page 157, *c* 20 quote various mdr. and mtr., without one single reference to Hayagrīva.

Page 157, *c* 22—page 158, *a* 28 correspond to Ts. 1056, page 73, *b* 3—*c* 10.

Page 158, *a* 29—*b* 7, compare Ts. 1056, page 74, *a* 5—13.

Page 158, *b* 8—*c* 2 contain mdr. and mtr., without any special bearing upon Hayagrīva.

Page 158, *c* 3—page 159, *b* 12, compare Ts. 1056 page 74, *a* 18—page 75, *a* 10.

Page 159, *b* 13—page 160, *a* 28 describe how by the inspection of various mystic syllables one may behold Vairocana, and the wonderful abode on top of the mount Meru. Here one will see at last a magnificent palace, where one may behold Hayagrīva. The ritual to be followed by the practitioner is described 160, *a* 28—*b* 14.

"Then in the middle of this palace one will see a lotus-flower. In the heart of this lotus-flower one should imagine the syllable *hrīḥ* [1]). It emanates a great effulgence, that illuminates all the boundless Buddha-worlds. All suffering creatures obtain salvation as soon as they are touched by this light. From this effulgence suddenly emerges the Great Fierce King Hayagrīva. He has four faces, all having a fierce expression. Tiger-teeth press the upper- and lower-lips. His eight hands all hold various weapons. He is sitting on a lotus-seat that rests on a flat rock. On top of his middle head there is a green horse's head. His hair is standing up loosely, like flames. The colour of his body is bright like the sun-disc. His body is entirely surrounded by flames, which excel the Fire of Universal destruction [2]). This fire consumes all the obstacles of Karma in men and gods. The crowds of fierce gods and the Ten Virtues of Perfection (personified) surround him as attendants. The Bs. of the Eight Offerings [3]) all occupy their places. At the four corners of the palace there are the four Mahākumāra's [4]), viz. Parātmā [5]), Paracana [6]), Ekajaṭārākṣasa [7]), and Aparati [8]). Each of them is on all sides surrounded by numberless attendants. The

1) Cf. *supra* page 51.

2) 劫災火, fire at the end of a Kalpa or world-period.

3) 八供養菩薩, cf. Mik., p. 1805.

4) ta-tung-tzŭ 大童子. 5) 婆羅跢麼(?) 6) 婆羅遮那(?).

7) 翳羅刹, cf. Mik. p. 72. 8) 阿婆羅底(?).

eight quarters are occupied by the Eight Great Dragon-Kings, together with the countless Dragon-Kings. And around these again, at the four sides, the twelve Great Heavenly Kings are standing. Their attendants are recruited from the eight classes of other gods. When one imagines the personal deity in this way, and the countless crowds of Holy One's, one should observe meticulous care, and not forget the correct order in which they all should be placed".

Finally a special mdr. and mtr. is described.

Page 160, *b* 25—page 161, *a* 26, compare Ts. 1056, page 75, *b* 12—page 76, *a* 27. In page 160, *c* 24 occurs a description of the Hook-mudrā of Hayagrīva, **馬頭尊鉤印**: both hands are folded together so as to form the Vajra-combination **金剛縛**. Both fore fingers are slightly bent, resembling a hook, pointing to one's body.

Page 161, *a* 27—*c* 9 quote various mdr. and mtr.

Page 161, *c* 10—15, compare Ts. 1056, page 76, *a* 28—*b* 4.

Page 161, *c* 16—23 quote a certain mdr. and mtr.

Page 161, *c* 24—page 162 *c* 5, compare Ts. 1056, page 76, *b* 6—page 77, *b* 15.

The first chapter closes with the description of a special offering (page 162, *c* 6—16).

SECOND CHAPTER

Page 163, *a* 5—page 164, *a* 10 give a description of the mdr. and mtr. which belong to the Ten Virtues of Perfection. Compare Ts. 1056, page 77, *b* 16—page 78, *b* 29.

Page 164, *a* 11—*b* 13 give the mdr. and mtr. of the Four Mahākumāra's, mentioned in the description of the Maṇḍala of Hayagrīva (see *supra* p. 88).

Page 164 *b* 14—page 165, *a* 2 quote the mdr. and mtr. of the Eight Great Dragon-Kings, mentioned above.

Page 165, *a* 2—*b* 19 enumerates the mdr. and mtr. of the Twelve Heavenly Kings: Īçvara, Indra, Agni, Yama, Rākṣasādhipati, Varuṇa, Vāyu, Vaiçravaṇa, Brahmā, Pṛthivi, Āditya and Candra.

Page 165, *b* 20—*b* 26 correspond to Ts. 901, page 803, *c* 5—11.

Page 165, *b* 27—*c* 4, cf. Ts. 901, page 833, *c* 18—23. Ts. 901, however, begins the mtr. with *oṁ*, instead of *namaḥ samanta buddhānām*.

Page 165, *c* 5—11, cf. Ts. 901, page 834, *a* 4—9. Again Ts. 901 has *oṁ* instead of *namaḥ* etc.

Page 165, *c* 12—17, cf. Ts. 901, page 834, *a* 16—22; again our text adds *namaḥ* etc. to the mtr.

Page 165, *c* 18—22, cf. Ts. 901, page 834, *b* 4—8; same remark as above.

Page 165, *c* 29—page 166, *a* 9, cf. Ts. 901, page 834 *b* 12—22.

Page 166, *a* 10—*b* 6 seem original; *a* 10—14 give a mdr. and mtr. for the devouring of all obstacles (諸障噉食印眞言); the mtr. is the same as quoted *supra*, page 65). A 14—26 describe mdr. and mtr. of the "Sharp sword that destroys all obstacles" (禁斷諸障銳刀), calling the fingers by their mystic names. The remaining text runs:

"The Holy, Great, Fierce King Hayagrīva. Now the most excellent basic mtr. (根本印) is explained: both hands are folded together, both fore-and ring fingers being bent, so that the backs of their nails touch each other inside the folded hands. The mdr. is then completed by erecting both thumbs. As soon as one has made this mdr. and chanted the mtr., this mdr. will send forth a great effulgence. Out of the mouth (formed by this mudrā?) there will come a Buddha of Transformation. All devils and non-Buddhist obstacles and all that have evil hearts will be dispersed, and take to flight hastily at the sight of this mdr. From the Ākāça-sphere above unto the Vāyu-sphere below, all the Vināyaka's that live in the air or dwell under the earth will have no power to do any harm. In the hearts of all of them Compassion is roused, and it will be impossible for them to do any mischief. Those that practise the mantra's and follow the discipline of a Bs., will not be hindered by obstacles and will obtain complete freedom. By making the mdr. and chanting the mtr. all these people will be entirely identified with the Great Fierce King".

Page 166, *b* 7—167, *a* 7, cf. Ts. 901, page 835, *c* 22—836, *c* 5.

Page 167, *a* 8—*a* 12 contain two mtr., that have no special bearing upon Hayagrīva.

Page 167, *a* 13—28 contain the Mantra of the Hundred Syllables of the Lotus-section 蓮華部百字眞言, and the magic successes to be derived from it.

Page 167, *a* 29—*b* 3 give another version of the rite described in Ts. 901, page 837, *a* 2—8.

Page 167, *b* 4—21 contain some original directions for the worship of Hayagrīva:

"Again the Mysterious Heart of the Holy Hayagrīva of Matchless and Unthinkable Strength is explained; (with his help) the methods for all kinds of rites can be effected.

One should chant the mtr. over vegetables, 100 000 times. Then one should during one day and one night abstain from all food; then only may one perform the Great Offering, and execute the Homa-rite[1]). One should burn 8000 twigs of a kind of sandal-

---

1) 護摩事業, the great Fire-offering, cf. Mik., p. 638 and Him., page 336.

wood [1]), both ends soaked in ghee. Then all the desires and hopes one cherishes in one's heart will be realised.

There is also another method: when one performs the Homa-rite 300 000 times with * * *-fruits [2]), then one will become a King [3]).

If one wishes to obtain a Great Manifestation, one should build in front of the image of Hayagrīva, an altar of four cubits square. In the middle of this altar one should place a pewter vessel, filled with perfumed water. From the first till the fifteenth day of the month, one should burn incense, scatter flowers and do homage and chant mtr. with great devotion. One should do this day and night, without sleeping a moment, strenuously keeping on without moving from one's place. When during fifteen days one has done so, without interruption, and having said the mtr. 500 000 times [4]), the Great Fierce King will manifest his Mysterious Body, and assist the practitioner. One will obtain the Great Abhijñā's [5]), and know thoroughly all things that exist in the Three Worlds. One will be well versed in all books that exist in this world, and know thoroughly all non-Buddhist methods and the Veda's.

Also if one should effect a Great Manifestation, one is then enabled to shake the mountains and rivers and stone walls, and stir the waters of the Four Great Oceans in the Trichiliomegachiliocosmos [6]). One can make the Sumeru and the Cakravāḍa-mountain tremble, and grind them to dust. And all living creatures that live thereon will be delivered from all pain and sorrow, and obtain great bliss, when they are touched by the light of this Great Fierce King".

Page 167, *b* 22—27, cf. Ts. 901, page 833, *c* 26—page 834, *a* 3.

Page 167, *b* 27—*c* 3, cf. Ts. 901, page 834, *a* 10—*a* 16. Our text adds at the end of the passage: "One will not suffer from disasters caused by heaven or earth, nor suffer from any sickness. One will obtain great magical success".

Page 167, *c* 4—7, cf. Ts. page 834, *a* 24—26.

Page 167, *c* 7—9 add: "Bad cold, fever, headache, pain in the feet, all the 404 sick-

---

1) 苦練木, cf. Mik., page 360. 2) 蜜攞嚩(?).

3) 惹 for 羅惹, S. *rājā*. 4) 五落叉, five *lakṣa*.

5) 神通, supernatural faculties. Usually six are enumerated: divine sight, divine hearing, the faculty of reading others' thoughts, the faculty of remembering one's former abodes or lives, the knowledge that transforms one's modes of life at will, the knowledge that destroys the impurities (Suzuki, page 383).

6) san-ch'ien-ta-ch'ien-shih-chieh 三千大千世界, cf. L. de la Vallée Poussin, Abhidharmakoça de Vasubandhu, Paris 1926, 3d chapter, p. 170.

nesses and the ten-thousand pains, they will all be cured. And the 80 000 sicknesses that are caused by devils, they will all be cured without exception, and one will obtain all magic success".

Page 167, *c* 9–16, cf. Ts. 901 page 834, *b* 23—29.

Page 167, *c* 16—20 are taken from Ts. 1214, a text devoted to Yamāntaka, where they are to be found on page 73, *b* 11—19. Two lines are added: through the magical power of the Great Fierce King all gods should obey the practitioner.

Page 167, *c* 22—25, cf. Ts. 901, page 836, *c* 13—15 [1]).

Page 167, *c* 25—page 168, *a* 13 are a mixture of lines taken from Ts. 1214 (page 73, *b* 14—20 and *a* 13—16), and of fragments referring to Hayagrīva. The text runs:

"There is another method in case there should be wicked people and enemies who plan to injure a good man. One should cast a bronze statue of the Fierce King; its size does not matter. This statue should have four faces and eight arms. The four faces each show sharp bare fangs. The eight hands show Vajra-weapons. The middle head wears on its crest a green horse's head. The hair on the head is standing upright like flames. Having an extremely fierce form he rides on a blue water-buffalo. On the back of this water-buffalo there is a lotus-flower, and thereon Hayagrīva is sitting with crossed legs. His whole body is surrounded by flames, which excel the fire of Universal Destruction. The Mysterious form of the Great Fierce King that subdues the enemies [2]) in the Three Worlds is like this. In front of this image one should make a triangular altar. On the base of this altar one should paint the body of the wicked man, or write his name thereon. The image of the god should be turned to the north, or also in the direction of the dwelling-place of the wicked man. Having chanted mantra's, one should put on black garments, and sit down with one's face turned to the image. In one's heart one should then rouse a great anger, and with a sharp voice recite mantra's, during three days and nights, each time for three hours. After these three days the wicked man will die, together with his whole family. If one should wish to bring him back to life, one should rouse great mercy in one's heart. Taking the root of a lotus-flower, one should pound it to dust. Then one should practise t h e s a m a y a o f t h e G r e a t M e r c y. During one day and one night one should neither eat nor drink. When one has repeated the mtr. one hundred an eight times,

---

1) The difficult character that indicates the kind of wood to be used (see *supra*, p. 68) is here replaced by c h ü n 俊; does 俊木 mean: "excellent wood"?

2) 設都嚧, S. *çatru*, cf. Buk., p. 807.

the wicked man and his family will be brought back to life; they will better themselves and adore Buddha and Dharma".

The passage closes with a special mdr. and mtr.

Page 168, *a* 14—21 correspond to Ts. 901, page 837, *b* 14—20; our text, however, begins the passage with: "In front of the image of Hayagrīva one should make a triangular altar; one should chant the mtr. 100 000 times. During three days and nights etc."

Page 168, *a* 21—*b* 7 seem original. The text runs:

"There is another method if all kinds of calamities and disasters should arise, and when the land would be in disorder; when resentful enemies in other countries plot an invasion, and make several attacks; when the people are discontented, and the ministers plan rebellion; when epidemics harass the land, when there are floods and droughts, and the regular course of sun and moon is broken: in a period of such general disaster, the King of this land should in all earnest ask a magician to chant mantra's in front of the image of the Great Fierce King. He should perform the Homa-rite 100 000 times with pumpkin-stalks [1]), soaked in ghee, milk and honey. Then the foreign enemies will submit, and all will declare their allegiance to the land, with a very humble heart they will turn to the King. The officials will all be loyal, and the queens and concubines will behave reverently to the King; all dragons, devils and ghosts will protect his land; rain will come down at the appropriate time, crops will be abundant, and the people will be happy.

There is another method if in one's household there should be a bad disease, and when many ominous signs appear; when ghosts and devils cause disorder, and when evil people in the house plot harm to each other by spreading calumnies. Without anyone, old or young, in the house itself or in the precincts knowing it, one should repeat mantra's in front of the image of Hayagrīva 100 000 times. Then all evil things will disappear completely.

There is another method when the officials of the King withold one's salary, and when one is thrown into jail, and put in irons. When one concentrates one's thoughts upon the Great Fierce King, the officials will on their own account again favour one, and set one free".

Page 168, *b* 7—21, cf. Ts. 901, page 837, *b* 21—*c* 6.

Page 168, *b* 21—23, cf. Ts. 901, page 836, *c* 21—23.

Page 168, *b* 23—*c* 4, cf. Ts. 901, page 837, *c* 7—19.

---

1) 滑(啗)瀘草. Cf. Mik., page 30.

Page 168, *c* 5—10 correspond to Ts. 901, Page 837, *c* 20—24 (see *supra*, page 73). Then, however, a different description is given of the image of the deity (*c* 10—21): "On this altar one should paint the Great Fierce King. He should have four faces, all wrathful, each face showing the bare fangs. The hair is standing upright like flames. Each head bears a heavenly cap, and the ears are adorned with jade-ornaments. On the heavenly cap a Buddha of Transformation is sitting with crossed legs. On the crest of the middle head there is a green horse's head, and the neck is adorned with beautiful ornaments. The colour of the body is resplendent like the sun-disc. The whole body is surrounded by a fire which excels the Fire of a Universal Destruction. He has eight arms. One left and one right hand are folded together so as to form the Secret Basic Mudrā of the Horse-mouth (cf. *supra*, p. 55). The next right hand holds a sharp sword, the next left hand carries the Vajra-staff. The next right hand holds the Vajra-axe, and the next left hand holds the Vajra-wheel. The next right hand makes the abhaya-mudrā (see *supra* page 69), the next left hand holds the Cintāmaṇi (see *supra*, page 70). The god is sitting on a flat rock, on a dais formed by a blue lotus-flower. The colour of the rock is just like that of a mountain, viz. a mixture of red, yellow and blue. All eight arms are adorned with wrist-rings and beautiful bracelets. The body is adorned in the same way as indicated in other places."

Page 168, *c* 22—page 169, *a* 14 correspond to Ts. 901, page 837, *a* 21—*b* 13. Our text, however, replaces in the sentence: "One will be born at the feet of Avalokiteçvara", the name Avalokiteçvara by Hayagrīva (see *supra*, page 70).

Page 169, *a* 15—*b* 20 contain a shortened version of the passage Ts. 901, page 838, *a* 17—26. Some lines in the description of the altar are changed, so as to make the description agree better with the maṇḍala of Hayagrīva, given above (see *supra*, page 88).

Page 169, *b* 21—*c* 7 are a curious mixture of various quotations, i. a. the passage of the Ta-jih-ching-shu (see *supra*, page 54).

Our text closes with detailed directions for making images of the Four Mahākumāra, and of the Eight Dragon Kings.

CHAPTER V

CONCLUSIONS

When we again look over the material concerning Hayagrīva collected in the foregoing chapters, it strikes us how in different areas this figure is connected with different conceptions. From this it is apparent that in the case under discussion as in most other cases, it is impossible to determine the significance of a god by one single formula.

For all that, in the semantic history of Hayagrīva an obvious trend is traceable: he is the specialized and therefore continually changing aspect of a great, essentially never changing, organic unity: the horse-cult. On account of his suggestive name, and his typical characteristic, the horse-head, Hayagrīva remained continually connected with this universal background. All varying aspects of the horse-cult found in him a form of expression.

When we regard Hayagrīva in this light, we are better enabled to understand his different significations. In countries where the horse-cult played a great part, Hayagrīva easily fitted in, and the cult of the horse itself was transferred to him. When this adaptation coincided with Buddhism becoming the dominating religion in one or another territory, there Hayagrīva won for himself a place in the foreground, and syncretistically or otherwise, incorporated local gods in his own person. We noticed that this has been the case in Tibet and in Mongolia, and, to a certain extent, also in Japan. In China, on the contrary, where in later times a special horse-cult had receded into the background, Hayagrīva remained a more or less theoretical figure, one of the many gods of the Mahāyānic Pantheon. But perhaps, a profound investigation, for instance in the North-west of China, where the breeding of horses is in the hands of a great part of the population, would bring to light the fact that here and there Hayagrīva enjoys special honour. In Peiping, on the 23d day of the sixth month, Ma-wang, the Ancestor of Horses, is worshipped by the owners of horses and carts, under the name of Shui-ts'ao-ming-wang 水草明王. This title appears to refer to Hayagrīva [1]).

The various magical conceptions with which Hayagrīva is associated, can all be deduced from the conspicuous physical characteristics of the horse.

---

1) Cf. W. Grube, Zur Pekinger Volkskunde, Berlin 1901, page 81.

In the first place, the function as fecundity-symbol, which is credited to the horse on account of phallic considerations. The identification of Hayagrīva and Viṣṇu, and the Açvamedha in general, belong to this category.

Secondly the neighing, the magical horse-voice. On one hand, this voice is melodious and well-omened: it is the sweet sound of Viṣṇu-Hayagrīva, promulgating the Sacred Word. On the other hand, it is the terrible sound that scares away devils: the Destroyer and Devourer, the bhairava Hayagrīva.

In the third place, its celerity: the horse is the swift charger, which carries his rider over the immeasurable plains. To this category belongs the idea of the divine, winged steed. In the "chest-nuts" or "scars" on the legs of the horse, one imagined to recognize the places where formerly the wings had been attached [1].

But it would be far too simplistic to deduce the origin of horse-cult only from these material data. The horse as symbol is deeply interwoven with the inner life of man. This is amply testified by dream-psychology; the tracing of this aspect of the problem, however, lies beyond the range of this study.

This paper bears only a preliminary and fragmentary character. All scientific work is doomed to be imperfect, but in re-reading these pages it could not but strike me how inadequate my knowledge and capacity appear in proportion to the breadth and depth of the subject I have undertaken to discuss. Several problems have only been touched upon, while I fain would have brought them to a satisfactory solution. I hope, however, that some of my observations may stimulate others, better qualified for this task, to a further research.

And in conclusion I hope that Mahābhārata II, 64, 8 may induce the reader to clemency, as it has brought solace to the writer, where it says:

................pravaṇād ivāmbho
yathā niyukto'smi tathā bhavāmi.

1) Cf. W. Crooke, The Popular Religion and Folklore of Northern India, London 1896, II, page 207.

ENDNOTES

P. 5, l. 5: "mantra-place"; the Tib. term is gzuṅs-bṣugs, litt. "dhāraṇī-place". Next to spell, dhāraṇī also means: the twelve qualities which uphold a Bs.

P. 47, l. 7 sq.: cf. also A. STEIN, Serindia, Vol. II (Text), p. 1087, where pictures of Chinese Buddhist Hells are described: ".... condemned souls wearing the cangue, driven along by ox- and horse-headed demons, who brandish goad and whip. Before them Kṣitigarbha, in a monks yellow robe and red mantle".

P. 50, l. 4: add the recent publication of Baron A. VON STAËL-HOLSTEIN: On two recent reconstructions of a Sanskrit hymn, transliterated with Chinese characters in the Xth century A.D., Peking 1934.

P. 56: to the shorter references may be added some passages occurring in other chapters of the T'o-lo-ni-chi-ching, e. g. ch. I, p. 790, *b*, and ch. IV, p. 816, *b*.

P. 80, l. 1: here should be mentioned also the two esoteric (*vajra*) appellations of Hayagrīva, viz. hsün-su-chin-kang "Swift Thunderbolt", and tan-shih-chin-kang "Devouring Thunderbolt". Hob., s. v. Batō, observes: "Ces noms paraissent reposer sur des interprétations fantaisistes du sc. *açva*, cheval, d'une part par *āçu*, rapide, de l'autre par *aç*, manger.

P. 80, l. 15 sq.: cf. also National Language Readers of Japan, Vol. VIII, 1931, p. 86, where wayside-offerings are described: "In front of the mound there stands a stone on which the Chinese characters Batō-Kanzeon are carved. Some new horse-shoes sometimes are offered before the stone. They say that pack-horse drivers offer these shoes so that their horses may not get hurt".

INDEX

(CHIEFLY PROPER NAMES, TITLES OF BOOKS, AND TECHNICAL EXPRESSIONS)

abhaya-mudrā 69, 94
ābhicārikāṇi 4
abhidharma 60
abhijñā 91
Açva 13
Açvaçankhu 13
Açvaçiras 10, 13, 15
Açvaçirṣa 10
Açvaghoṣa 46
Açvagrīva 13, 15
Açvamedha 10, 96
Açvamukha 10, 47
Açvapati 13
Açvaratna 23, 24, 29, 45, 54, 55
āditya 10
Āditya 89
Aerial Horse 29, 46
agaru-perfume 75
Agni 14, 89
Agni-purāṇa 18
āḥ, the syllable, 30
Airāvata 10
Ajita 56
Ākāça-sphere 90
Akṣobhya 33, 34, 81
ālaya-vijñāna 86
Amitābha 29, 31
Amoghapāça 24, 39, 65
Amoghavajra 25—27, 34, 52, 55, 63, 81, 82
Āmra-wood 27
amṛta 85
amṛtodbhava 10, 11, 55, 64
Andersson, J. G. 43
an-hsi-hsiang 68
añjali 53, 62, 63, 64
añjana 70
antara-bandhana 53
Anuruddhamokṣa 59
Ao, Prince 58, 60
Arjuna 10
Aston, W. G. 76—78, 80
asura 13, 16, 17, 32, 71
Atharva-veda 4
Atīça 36, 37
Ātmarakṣa 62, 69, 73
Aurva 11
Auryānala 11
Avalokiteçvara 23, 24, 28, 35, 39, 40, 46, 51, 54, 55, 62, 65, 67, 69, 70, 79, 94
Avalokiteçvara, Eight-armed 74, 75
Avalokiteçvara-with-thousand-eyes-and-hands 82, 83
Avalon, A. 3, 51

Bacot, J. 23, 29
Badarī 10
bahir-bandhana 53
Balāha 23, 24, 29, 46
Basic Mudrā of Hayagrīva 94
Batōkannon-shindarani 84
Bdellion 98
Bhadra-kalpa 23
Bhāgavata-purāṇa 17, 18
bhairava 21, 22, 29, 38, 39, 96
Bhaktamālā 18, 19
Bhartṛmeṇṭha 20
Bhīma 13
Bhṛkuṭī 39, 40, 54, 62
bīja 51, 82
Bodhi 85
Bodhicitta 87
Bodhimaṇḍa 74, 87
Bodhirṣi 56
Bodhiruci 24, 56
Bodhisattva's-of-the-Eight-Offerings 88
Bodhisattva-with-eleven-faces 74, 75
Bosch, F. D. K. 17
Brahmā, 7, 11—14, 17, 18, 32,
Brahmaloka 12
Brandes, 39
Buddha of Transformation 69, 73, 90, 94; v. *hua-fu*

Çaiva-siddhānta 3
Cakravāḍa-mountain 91
Cakravartin 11, 23, 32, 54, 70
çakti 37
Çāktism 22
Çākyamuni 23
Çambhara 13, 15, 17
Candra 89
Çaṅkara 32
Çankha 71
Çankhapāla 74
çapharī-fish 17
Ceka-land 27
Chakravarti, G. 22
Challaye, F. 79
Charpentier, J. 9
Chavannes, E. 23
Ch'eng-huang 47
Cheng-yüan-hsin-ting-shih-chiao-mu-lu 26, 57, 82
chen-shui 75
chia-ma 46
chien-ku-chieh 55
ch'ih-ma 46
Chih Sheng 57

Ch'i-lin 29, 45
Ching-hsing-monastery 59
Chin-kang-ta-tao-ch'ang-ching 59, 61
Chin-kang-ting-yu-ch'ieh-ch'ien-shou-ch'ien-yen kuan-tzŭ-tsai-p'u-sa-hsiu-hsing i-kuei-ching 82
Chou-dynasty 41
Chou-halberds 38
Chou-li 41, 42
Ch'uang-tzŭ 42
Chu Hsi 45
Ch'un-ch'iu 43
Cintāmaṇi 23, 70, 94
Çītalā 40
Çiva 14, 21, 22, 28, 29, 32, 67
Cohn, W. 39, 40
Confucius 45
Coomaraswamy, A. K. 7
Cordier, P. 30, 33
Çrāvastī 61
Çrīdhara 18
Çrīmitra 28
Crooke, W. 96
Csoma de Körös, A. 48
Çubhākarasiṁha 25, 26, 27, 47, 54
Çuddhāvāsa-gods 74

Dadhīca 17
Dadhikrā(van) 9
Daihyakkajiten 77, 78, 79
Danu 13, 15, 17
Das, S. C. 34, 38
Dattātreya 19
Devībhāgavata-purāṇa 18
Dharmacakra-mudrā 85
Dharmagupta 26
dharma-pāla 28
dharma-paryāya 59
Djago, tjandi 39
Digambara-sect 32
Doré, H. 45—47
drag-gçed 28
dragon 41, 42
Dragon-Horse 29, 45
Dragon-King 74, 75, 89, 94
Dumont, P. E. 10
Duryodhana 13
Dutt, N. 26

Eckardt 47
Eggeling 20
Ekajaṭārākṣasa 88
Elixir of Immortality 32
ema 77—79
ema-dō 78
Entsūji 80

Fang-su 41
Fan-i-ming-i-chi 87
Fan-yü-tzŭ-tien 70
fen-nu-ch'uan 53
Forest, J. H. de 78
Francke, A. H. 48
Fuchs, W. 59
Fujiwara, A. 78
Fukū 27

gandhanakuli-flower 70
gaṇḍī 87
Gaṇeça 7, 68
Ganges 12
Garuḍa 29, 38
Goçīrṣa 47
Goloka 12
Goloubew, V. 23
gorocanā 64
Gravely 19, 21
Grierson 19
Grube, W. 95
guggulu-perfume 68
Güntert, H. 9

Hachiman 80
Hackin, J. 23
Hajo 22, 29
haṁ, the syllable 30, 31, 34, 51
Hari 14, 17, 18, 32
Hatsusegawa-temple 78
Hattori 54
Hayaçiras 14, 19
Hayaçīrṣa 10, 18
Hayaçīrṣa-pañcarātra 20
Hayagrīva-Mādhava 22, 29
Hayagrīva-mahāmantra 22
Hayagrīva-sahasrākṣaramahāmantra 22
Hayagrīva-stotra 20
Hayagrīva-upaniṣad 20
Hayagrīva-vadha 20
Hayāsya 18
Heavenly Kings, Twelve Great 89
Hemādri 20
Hentze, C. 45
Hiraṇyakaçipu 17—19
ho-chang 53, 62
homa-rite 90, 91, 93
Honchōmonsui 78
hook-mudrā of Hayagrīva 89
Hopkins, W. 5, 11
hrīḥ, the syllable 32, 51, 88
Hsi-t'an-tzŭ-chi 48
Hsi-yu-chi 45
Hsüan K'ai 57—59
Hsüan Tsang 26, 27, 45
hua-fu 55, 69; v. *Buddha of Transformation*
Huber, E. 23
Hui-jih-monastery 57—61
Hui Kuo 25, 27, 79
Hui Li 27
hūṁ, the syllable 30, 32, 33, 51, 63, 64, 67, 85

Īçānavarman 26
Ichigyō 26
Īçvara 89
Ihm, H. 76, 77
I Hsing 25—27, 54
I-li 43
Indra 11, 16, 17, 89

iṣṭadevatā 87
Itsukushima-temple 79

Jaina 32
Jitsu-e 79
jñāna 31, 52
Jōgon 82
Johansson, K. F. 9
ju-lai-ch'uan 53
Julien, Stanislas 50

Kaçyapa 15
Kaçyapa (priest) 59
Kaiṭabha 11, 13, 14, 19
K'ai-yüan-shih-chiao-mu-lu 57
Kālidāsa 5
Kālikā-purāṇa 22
Kalpa (world-period) 17, 23, 88
Kalpa (ritual) 81
Kaṁsa 16
K'ang-hsi-tzŭ-tien 63
Kansōzuihitsu 77
Kaṇṭhaka 22
Kanzeonji 80
kapiça-incense 71
karaṇa-mudrā 34, 35
Karaṇḍavyūha 23
Karkoṭaka 74
Karlgren, B. 41, 43, 50
kāṣāya 73
Kat Angelino, P. de 51
Kātantra 3
Kawamoura 51
Kayakiribazōhō 84
Kayakiribakanzeombosatsuju-hōdan 84
Keçin 13—17
Keika 27
Khadira-wood 38, 71, 72
khaṁ, the syllable 51
Khasarpaṇa 40
kīla 37
Kirfel, W. 15
Kiyomizu-temple 78
Kōbō Daishi 79
Komatsubara, Kannon-temple at 80
Kongōchi 26
Koppers, W. 9
koṭanaka 87
Krishna Sastri 20
krodha-muṣṭi 35, 53
Krom, N. J. 36
kris 38
Kṛṣṇa 12, 13, 16
Kṛtanagara 39
Kubera 67
kuçala-mūla 86
Ku-chin-t'u-shu-chi-ch'eng 45
kuda-sembrani 38
Kūkai 79
Kulika 74
Kunadō 80
kunduruka-perfume 75
Kuo Mo-jo 41
Kuo P'o 41

Lakṣmī-devī 59
Lakṣmīnarasiṁha-temple 21
lalitakṣepa-attitude 33
Lañtsha-characters 48
Laufer, B. 45
Lévi, Sylvain 50, 78
Leyden Museum 36, 38, 39, 79
Li-chi 43—45
Li-ch'ü-chiao 86
lien-hua-ch'uan 53
liu-chung-ch'uan 53
Li Shih-chi 58
Lotus-section 54, 79, 90
Lung-ma 29, 45
Lung-nao 64

Macchandar Vahal 35
Macdonell 9
Madhu 11, 13, 14, 19
Mahābalaguṇa 56
Mahābodhi-monastery 59
Mahākumāra, Four 88, 89, 94
Mahāmāyūrīvidyārājñī 28
Mahāpadma 74
Mahāvairocana-sūtra 24, 28, 54
Mahāvidyārāja 55
Maheçvara 67
maithuna 22
Maitreya 23, 32, 33
Mallitamma 21
Ma-mien 47
manaḥçila 70
maṇḍala 6, 24, 39, 54, 73, 75, 87
maṇḍala of Hayagrīva 82, 89, 94
Mañjuçrī 56
Mantra-piṭaka 61
ma-pao 54
Māra 85
Mārīcī 37
Maruts 14
Maspéro, G. 47
Ma-t'ou 47
Ma-t'ou-niang 46
Matsuodera 80
Ma-wang 95
Meru-mountain 11, 88
Milloué, de 51
Ming Ch'uan 57
Mohinī 19
Müller, S. 9
Muru 15

Nābhādāsa 18
Nachod, O. 76, 77
Nāgabodhi 25—27
Nāgarāja 74
Nāgārjuna 25—27
Nālandā 26, 39
Nanda 74
Nanjō, B. 83
Nara 10
Nārada 10, 11
Naraka 15
Nārāyaṇa 10, 11, 13, 67
Nārāyaṇīyamantrarahasya 22

Naya-doctrine 86
nei-fu 53
Nisunda 15
niu-huang 64
Niu-t'ou 47

Oḍra 25
Oe Tadahira 78
Oldenburg, S. 36, 37
oṁ, the syllable 12, 30, 32, 34, 51, 55, 62—64, 85, 89

Padma 74
Padmanarteçvara 40
padma-muṣṭi 53
Padma Thang Yig 37
Pañcanāda 15
Pañcarātrāgama 20, 21
Pañcatantra 1, 3
Paraçu-rāma 19
Paramāçva 24
Paramāçvavajra 34
pāramitā 52, 86
parittā 25
Parṇaçavarī 40
Pārvatī 22
Patālā 10
Pa-tzŭ-wen-shu-kuei 56
P'ei-wen-yün-fu 58
Pelliot, P. 58
phaṭ, the syllable 32, 51, 63, 64, 67, 68, 85
phur-bu 37
Piao-chih-chi 26
Pṛthivi 89
Przyluski, J. 25, 29
Pu-k'ung-chuan-so-shen-pien-chen-yen-ching 56
Puloman 13, 15, 17
Pūṣan 16
P'u-t'i-ch'ang-so-shuo-i-tzŭ-ting-lung-wang-ching 55

Rājataraṅginī 20
Rākṣasādhipati 89
Rāma 16, 19
Ramacandra 19
Rāmānuja 18
Rāmarāmavivāda 19
Rao, Gopinath 18, 19
realgar 70
Ṛg-veda 4, 9
rluṅ-rta 29, 46
Roerich, G. de 37
Rñiṅ-ma-sect 37
Rosenberg, O. 50
rta-mchog 28
rta-mgrin 28, 35
Rudra 37
Ryūchi 26

saddharma 86
sādhana 30, 33, 34, 38, 84
Samantabhadra 26
samaya 87, 92
saṁgīti 61
saṁkakṣika 73
sandal-perfume 75
sandal-wood 90
Saptaçatikakalpa 29—33
sapta-ratnāni 11, 23
Sarasvatī 12
sarjarasa-incense 71
Satow 76, 77
Satyā 14
Satyavrata 18
sayādhi-devatā 87
Schlagintweit 5, 29
Schmidt, H. 79
Sheng-yen-man-te-chia-wei-nu-wang li-ch'eng ta-shen-yen nien-sung-fa 83
She-ta-i-kuei 52
She-wu-ai-ching 55
Shih-ching 42
Shih-erh sheng-chiang 47
Shih-i-chi 45
Shimotodachi-festival 77
Shin-ga 79
Shingon 8, 79, 80, 81
Shintō 8, 76—80
Shishimuikanzeon 80
Shōkayakiribadaiinuō ryūjō daishinken kuyōnenju gikihōbon 81; analysis 85
Shu-ching 45
Shui-ts'ao-ming-wang 95
Shurhammer 79
Siddhaṁ-characters 48, 49, 84
Siddhārtha 23
siddhi 61, 71, 75, 85
sīmabandhana 62
Siṁhala 23, 24
Siṁhaladvīpa 24
Skandha 67
Sku lṅa 36
Staël-Holstein, Bar. A. von 50, 87
Sudhanakumāra 39
Sukhāvatī 70
sumana-flower 63
Sumeru-mountain 30, 91
Sung-kao-seng-ch'uan 25—27, 57, 63
Sung-ti-wang 46
surabhi-flower 69
Susa-no-o 76
suvarṇa 10, 72
Suzuki, D. T. 86, 91
Suzuki, T. 77

Ta-chou-k'an-ting-chung-ching-mu-lu 57
Ta-jih-ching-shu 54, 94
Takada 44
Takahashi, G. 38
Takṣaka 74
T'ang-shu 58
Tārā 39, 54
Tārakā-battle 15, 16
Tārkṣya 9
Ta-sheng-tsung 58, 60
tathāgata-muṣṭi 53
Tendai-sect 80

Toussaint, G. C. 37
Trailokavijaya 56
tripatāka-mudrā 34
Ts'an-ming 46
Tung Chün 42
Tz'ŭ-en-chuan 26
Tz'ŭ-en-monastery 58
Tz'ŭ-yüan 46

ū, the syllable 51, 63, 64, 85
Uccaiḥçravas 10, 11, 23
Uke-mochi-no-kami 76
unicorn 29, 45
Usakajinja 77

Vaḍavāmukha 10, 11, 67, 68
Vaiçravaṇa 89
Vairocana 5, 25, 27, 51, 88
Vajrabodhi 25—27, 81
Vajraçekharasūtra 26, 82
vajramuṣṭi 53
Vajrapāṇi 81, 85
Vajrasattva 25—27, 81
Vajravārāhī 37
Vālāha 46
Vallée Poussin, L. de la 3, 91
vaṁ, the syllable 51
Vāmana 17
Varuṇa 14, 89
Vasuki 74
Vāyu 89
Vemacitra 32
Veṅkaṭanātha 20
Vidyādhara 24, 25, 29, 32, 70
Vidyādhararāja 24
Vidyādharī 25
Vidyārāja 24, 25, 28, 54—56, 83
Vikramorvaçī 5
Vinaya 60
Vināyaka 68, 70, 90
Viṣṇu 10—22, 24, 28, 29, 67, 96
Viṣṇu-purāṇa 16, 17
Viṣṇuvardhana 39
vitasti 69, 73
Vṛndā-wood 16
Vṛtra 17

Waddell 25, 28, 29
Wahle, E. 9
wai-fu 53
Waley, Arthur 78
Walleser 26
Wang Chia 45
Wasudev Laxman 20
Watanabe 77
Weber 79
Wei-ch'ih Ching-te 58
Wen Wang 43
Wilson, H. H. 16
Wish-granting Gem 23, 32, 45, 70, 73
Wish-granting Tree 32
Wogihara 48
Woodroffe, Sir John 3
Wu-liang-shou-ju-lai-kuan-hsing-kung-yang-i-kuei 55

Yama 46, 89
Yamada, T. 50
Yamāntaka 83, 92
Yāska 9
Yen-lo-wang 46, 47
yi-dam 35
Ying, Prince 58, 60
Yoginī-tantra 22
Yüan Chao 57
Yudhiṣṭhira 12

www.ingramcontent.com/pod-product-compliance
Ingram Content Group UK Ltd.
Pitfield, Milton Keynes, MK11 3LW, UK
UKHW050415240426
12048UKWH00021B/1528

9 789745 241565